WITHDRAWN

The BIG SIX

The Selling Out of America's Top Accounting Firms

MARK STEVENS

Research by Carol Bloom Stevens

SIMON & SCHUSTER

New York London Toronto Sydney Tokyo Singapore

Simon & Schuster
Simon & Schuster Building
Rockefeller Center
1230 Avenue of the Americas
New York, New York 10020

Designed by Chris Welch
Manufactured in the United States of America

1 3 5 7 9 10 8 6 4 2

Library of Congress Cataloging in Publication Data
Stevens, Mark, date
The big six : the selling out of America's top accounting firms /
Mark Stevens ; research by Carol Bloom Stevens.
p.   cm.
Includes index.
1. Accounting firms—United States—Corrupt practices.
2. Consolidation and merger of corporations—United States.   3. Big
business—United States.   I. Stevens, Carol Bloom.   II. Title.
III. Title: Big 6.
HF5616.U5S754   1991
338.7′61657′0973—dc20   91-8914
                                                           CIP

ISBN 0-671-69549-5

Opening quotes from chapters 2, 3, 4, 5, and 6 come from *The Pocket Book of
Quotations*, edited by Henry Davidoff and published by Pocket Books, a division of
Simon & Schuster, 1230 Avenue of the Americas, New York, NY 10020, copyright
1942, 1952 by Simon & Schuster Inc.

To Minnie and Izzie . . . the best there ever were

Contents

The

BIG

SIX

PROLOGUE

The names have become synonymous with the worst in American business: ZZZZ Best, Beverly Hills Savings & Loan, Penn Square Bank, Lincoln Savings & Loan. In case after case, sordid episode after sordid episode, companies and institutions regarded as mainstays of the capitalist system have disintegrated overnight, brought to their knees by reckless management, a crazy quilt of questionable financial practices and, in some instances, outright fraud.

That senior corporate executives would be guilty of Machiavellian greed and ambition is distressing. But even more distressing is the fact that so many of the major corporate disasters of recent years have occurred right under the "watchful eyes" of the premier accounting firms in the nation: the Big Six. For this reason, scandals of such magnitude must be viewed as more than extraordinary flimflams. Behind the headlines and the balance sheets, they reveal shocking examples of the Big Six's power and influence—and how that power and influence is used and abused.

The Big Six are the successors to the Big Eight, the group of practices that dominated public accounting until the 1989 megamergers uniting Ernst & Whinney with Arthur Young and Touche Ross with Deloitte Haskins & Sells reduced the oligopoly to six firms, concentrating their power further.

Today, the Big Six include Arthur Andersen, KPMG Peat Marwick, Ernst & Young, Coopers & Lybrand, Price Waterhouse and Deloitte & Touche. Ranked by 1989 revenues and number of partners, they stack up as shown on the opposite page.

Although the firms are often lumped together under the heading "the Big Six," each has a distinct corporate culture and personality.

Arthur Andersen: The firm the others love to hate, Big Arthur is a curious mixture of a modern marketing machine and a hidebound professional practice so certain of its superiority that it looks condescendingly on all those outside its Chicago fortress. The culture is early IBM, with white shirts, rep ties and anonymous suits the required uniform. This has bred a corps of humorless stuffed-shirt managers now struggling to guide the firm through a turbulent period. They may find that the worst is yet to come.

Major clients include Texaco, GTE, Tenneco, Georgia-Pacific, Colgate-Palmolive and International Paper.

KPMG Peat Marwick: A powerhouse in the banking industry, Peat has absorbed a major merger with a large second-tier firm, Main Hurdman. After a bloody period during which substantial numbers of Main Hurdman partners were cut from the ranks, Peat hoped to get back into a growth mode. But recent revenues have been flat, as reflected in the announcement that 265 additional partners would be dismissed in 1991. Although the firm scored a major coup in securing the PepsiCo audit (after Ernst & Young was forced to relinquish it because of a conflict with Coca-Cola), there are weaknesses in the House of Peat. The vaunted KPMG international network does not always perform like a cohesive unit, and Peat's plan to set itself off with Arthur Andersen as the Big Two has been thwarted

Two mergers in 1989 reduced the Big Eight accounting firms to the Big Six.

Ernst & Young

$1.32	$.94	$2.26
1,260	871	2,131

Ernst & Whinney + Arthur Young

Arthur Andersen

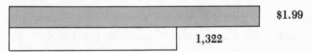

$1.99

1,322

Deloitte & Touche

$.93	$.92	$1.85
807	845	1,652

Touche Ross + Deloitte Haskins & Sells

KPMG Peet Marwick

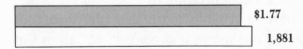

$1.77

1,881

Coopers & Lybrand

$1.28

1,252

*Source:
Bowman's
Accounting
Report*

Price Waterhouse

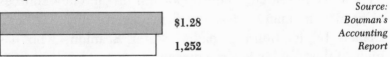

$1.10

845

Revenues for
fiscal 1989
in billions

Partners

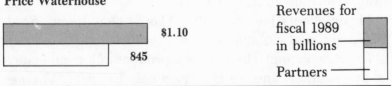

by the megamergers that produced Ernst & Young and Deloitte & Touche.

The atmosphere at Peat is highly charged and extremely political.

Major clients include PepsiCo, General Electric, Citicorp, Manufacturers Hanover, US AIR, Aetna Life & Casualty, Xerox, Union Carbide, J. C. Penney and the City of New York.

Price Waterhouse: Stuffy and successful, PW considers itself the elite firm and has ammunition to back it up: highest partner earnings in the Big Six and more blue-chip *Fortune* 100 clients than any other firm. But in many ways, PW is trading on past glories. Its lingering white-shoe culture is out of place in the modern market for consulting services. As mergers have shrunk PW's premier client base, and as a new breed of CFOs has solidified its power at the blue chips, its long-term relationships with its clients have been threatened. The firm's image has also been damaged by two aborted merger attempts.

Major clients include IBM, USX, Borden, J. P. Morgan, du Pont, W. R. Grace, Hewlett-Packard, Walt Disney, Bristol-Myers, Shell Oil and Gannett.

Coopers & Lybrand: Highly aggressive, the firm is at the cutting edge of marketing and consulting. Always at the frontier of new services, it has expanded the scope of its practice in search of new opportunities (and new sources of profit). In many ways, the firm's personality has been shaped by its bulldog leader, Peter Scanlon, who has bucked the trend in favor of megamergers but has benefited from defections in other camps.

Major clients include CBS, AT&T, Dow-Jones, Ford, Firestone, and Goldman-Sachs.

Ernst & Young: The firm is a product of a combination of two cautious and starchy practices, Ernst & Whinney and Arthur Young. Although the union was touted as a merger, evidence indicates that the transaction was an acquisition in disguise, with the stronger Ernst & Whinney gobbling up Young. Both firms have fortress mentalities (which resent meddling by the press) and are strongest in the classic audit practice.

Major clients include Coca-Cola, American Express, Mobil Oil, McDonnell Douglas, Apple Computer, and Unisys.

Deloitte & Touche: The firm is a product of a merger between strange bedfellows, Deloitte Haskins & Sells and Touche Ross, which, on the surface, appeared to be polar opposites. Traditionally, Deloitte's culture has been that of a slow-and-steady "auditor's auditor"—a far cry from Touche's reputation as an aggressive practitioner hell-bent on violating big-firm etiquette. But under a new generation of managing partners who rose to power in the mid-1980s (Mike Cook at Deloitte and Ed Kangas at Touche), the firms have become kindred spirits. Today, these hard-nosed bottom-liners are shaping the personality of Deloitte & Touche.

Major clients include General Motors, Merrill Lynch, Chrysler, Procter & Gamble, Metropolitan Life, Kohlberg Kravis & Roberts, *The New York Times*, Sears Roebuck, Prudential and Boeing.

For decades, the Big Eight (now the Big Six) have basked in the prestige of the corporate world's most exclusive fraternity. Being a Big Six firm, like going to an Ivy League college, has implied superiority. To company CEOs, CFOs and audit committees that hire them and pay them fortunes in accounting and consulting fees, the Big Six have long been considered the only professionals capable of serving multinational corporations, a bias that translates into money, power, position and clout—all reinforcing their mystique.

Like other power brokers in America, the Big Six have remained secretive in their ways. Cloaked by the shroud of "professionalism" and the confidentiality of client-accountant relationships, the firms have camouflaged the true nature of their practices. But in recent years, cross-currents moving throughout the top end of the profession have converged to reshape the firms and their practice dramatically—and to bring the glare of unwelcome publicity to the *way* they practice.

Tracing their origins to chartered accountants from the United Kingdom who first came to the United States in the nineteenth century to oversee the commercial interests of British industrialists and entrepreneurs, the Big Six have emerged during the twentieth century as behemoth professional firms with nearly ten thousand partners among them and aggregate revenues exceeding $16 billion worldwide. As the independent auditors to the blue chips of U.S. business and industry, they have earned a reputation of being the world's premier accountants, a reputation that during an earlier chapter in their history was well deserved—but no more. Today accounting is suffering a major identity crisis, both in the way it is viewed by the public it is supposed to serve and in the way it views itself.

Much of the malaise in the Big Six can be traced to a massive reshaping of the firms during the past decade. While all have clung to their heritage of "certified public accountants," a close look reveals that they are no longer accounting firms but instead are broad-based consulting practices serving an interlocking network of corporate, governmental and institutional clients from *Fortune* 500 aerospace contractors to Hollywood studios to the U.S.

Congress. Whether the design and installation of massive computer systems, feasibility studies for metropolitan airports or strategies for shrinking corporate and governmental debt are involved, the Big Six play a critical role, defining options for managers, politicians and technocrats.

But as consulting has grown from 25 percent to more than 40 percent (depending on the firm) of Big Six revenues and the lion's share of profits, open warfare has erupted between the auditors (the traditional overlords of the Big Six) and the consultants (the new heirs to the throne). In fact, emotions have run so high at Chicago-based Arthur Andersen that a besieged management has divided the giant firm into two separate, semiautonomous divisions. But even that dramatic move may have failed to solve the greater issue of how accountants and consultants are to coexist and what, if anything, the firms can do to hold together the two critical (but often conflicting) components of their far-flung practices.

Even beyond the bubbling animosity between consultants and auditors, there are the hard-and-fast limitations of operating a successful consulting practice within the confines of a public accounting firm. As independent consulting firms not tied to the accounting profession have moved toward joint ventures with their clients, most Big Six consultants find themselves hamstrung by professional ethics forbidding such intimate relationships. What's more, as accounting firms have been whipsawed by costly legal battles often resulting in multi-million-dollar settlements (including huge payments to savings and loan investors), consultants have been embittered by the specter of the fees they are generating being sucked into the black hole of audit litigation. Increasingly, they are yearning for a more independent, laissez-faire environment where they can pursue their professional objectives without the excess baggage of the auditor's restraints and liabilities. The widening schism between the audit and consulting practices has brought bad blood between accountants and consultants throughout the Big Six. Behind the scenes, the firms are hardly the models of collegiality and fraternity their high-powered public relations agencies seek to convey.

As they have transformed themselves from number crunchers into mass-market think tanks, and as they have added tens of thousands of partners and staff to their ranks, the Big Six have been forced to scour the marketplace for new sources of revenue to cover upwardly spiraling overheads, an objective that has grown in urgency as the firms' traditional meat-and-potatoes business, the annual audit of *Fortune* 500 companies, has been subjected to cutthroat competition and, in turn, to declining fees. "Gone are the days when the giant audit firms could get anything close to their standard hourly rates for staff or partner services," says Richard Eisner, managing partner of a New York–based firm that bears his name. "In cases where we compete with them, we see the Big Six charging rates as low as 50 cents on the dollar. Better than anything else, that shows how far they've fallen and how desperate they are for business."

To complicate matters, a new, hard-boiled generation of corporate financial officers has moved away from hiring auditors on the basis of old school ties, subjecting them instead to rigorous evaluations and in many cases to competitive bidding. For this reason, the Big Six have lost the hammerlock on major clients that once assured them of a steady stream of revenues. Clients that had retained a Price Waterhouse or Peat Marwick for generations—believing they were the best to do the job—are now inviting all of the giants to compete for the audit, the prize going to the lowest bidder. Suddenly the audit is a commodity, and to compete, the Big Six can no longer hold out for the astronomical fees once taken for granted.

As if declining fees weren't bad enough, changes in professional ethics have dealt a deathblow to the audit world as the firms once knew it. Ever since the American Institute of Certified Public Accountants lifted a longtime ban on accountants' soliciting or advertising for business, the Big Six have employed an arsenal of marketing tactics including advertising, public relations, sales promotions and sales training, all designed to pirate business from one another. In the process, they have sought to transform their partners from archetypal Caspar Milquetoasts—who entered the profession specifically because it offered them a safe harbor from the selling required in other fields—into an army of Ed (publishers' sweepstakes) McMahons. This has sent shock waves through the system, forcing partners to generate a minimum level of fees or face being routed from the ranks. To a generation of CPAs nurtured on the concept "Once a partner, always a partner," it has been a bitter pill to swallow.

Although the firms are loath to admit it, partnership in a Big Six firm today carries little more clout or status than that of a corporate employee. Behind the pin-striped curtain, Darwinian selection has replaced the traditional emphasis on fraternity and collegiality. Long gone is the once-cherished notion that partners take care of their own. In the current bottom-line environment, it is "every man for himself."

While a meritocracy may be appropriate in most businesses (where selling in one form or another is the name of the game), CPA firms are unlike most businesses. Licensed to audit public companies and in effect to serve as watchdogs of the public interest, they have a duty that extends beyond the profit motive. Above all else, the opinions they render must be accurate, independent and above reproach. The nation's financial system, in fact capitalism as we know it, relies on this. But as salesmanship has been elevated over technical prowess and some of the best minds have been pushed into the bowels of the organization because they cannot charm clients into the fold, the quality and accuracy of the firms' opinions has to suffer.

To observers of the Big Six, the great cause for alarm today is that they are ostracizing a group critical to quality work: the good, fastidious CPAs who cross their "t's" and dot their "i's" but who can't market, sell or promote themselves to clients. These practitioners are being expelled from the ranks, victims of the blind drive toward greater profitability. The effect of this bottom-line myopia is painfully clear: The National Commission on Fraudulent Financial Reporting has found that fee and budget pressures detract from audit quality, making it possible for fraud to slip by undetected.

"Intense competition among accounting firms contributes to significant pressure on audit fees, often with corresponding pressure to reduce staff, time budgets, and partner involvement in audit engagements," the commission reports. "Such pressures may not be conducive to the thorough investigation of red flags indicating the potential for fraudulent financial reporting, or to the thorough exercise of professional judgment and skepticism."

Underlying all of the changes in the Big Six is a fundamental revision in the way they view themselves. For generations, members of these huge, influential practices considered themselves professionals who happened to be in business. But beginning in the 1980s, this view flip-flopped: Increasingly, they saw themselves as businessmen who happened to be professionals. The distinction is critical. To professionals, ethics are the foundation on which their practices are based. But to businessmen, ethics have always been a side issue, to be ignored or observed depending on the executives and the circumstances they found themselves in. That CPAs began to see themselves more as businessmen than as professionals has had a profound impact on their performance as "financial watchdogs." "They're supposed to be professional firms," said Steve Oppenheim, former chairman of the now defunct midsize CPA firm of Spicer & Oppenheim, "and for professional firms to preserve their integrity, they have to be willing to boot out questionable clients, no matter what that does to the bottom line. And there's the rub. Considering that the firms are now obsessed with growth—and are filling their ranks with people who know how to sell— who's left to do the booting out? Look, the Six-Pack aren't bad people. But they have to recognize that when you skew the economics to reward a certain type of behavior, that's the type of behavior you'll get."

"The firms have moved from being product-oriented to being market-oriented," says Jay Nisberg, a consultant specializing in the management of professional firms. "That move has created a great deal of confusion internally. In the past, when the primary objective was to provide a quality product—be it in tax, audit or consulting—all the partners knew their role: To do their work as competently and as effectively as possible. But now that the gears have switched to marketing and selling, the partners are experiencing an identity crisis. 'What's my job supposed to be?' they wonder. 'Is it to develop people, to audit, to be a public speaker, to recruit, to sign up clients?' Many don't know." The question is, how far can the Big Six stray from their traditional mission as auditors of public corporations and their traditional culture of being high-minded professional firms without jeopardizing the position of trust and confidence that has long been their greatest asset? Privately, many in the profession share that concern. They fear that the Big Six's aggressiveness, their departure from once-sacrosanct traditions and their adventures into an ambitious range of practice disciplines will prompt clients to alter their perception of CPAs from that of prudent, conservative professionals to that of opportunistic entrepreneurs whose signatures at the end of a financial statement are as meaningful as a rubber stamp.

The megamergers that have transformed the Big Eight into the Big Six are not isolated events. Instead, they are symbolic of the many profound changes that have been reshaping the accounting giants, changes that have clouded their perception, diminished their professionalism, generated bitter internal conflict and made possible financial debacles that have shocked the nation. From any standpoint, this is a profession in crisis.

1

THE ZZZZ BEST
CASE

Don't Blame Us, We're Only Accountants

This case shows that unless crooks undergo a character transformation and rat on themselves, there is a good chance that they won't be caught wrecking publicly held corporations until great damage is done.

—REP. RONALD WYDEN
HOUSE SUBCOMMITTEE ON OVERSIGHT AND INVESTIGATIONS

Back in the early 1980s, Barry J. Minkow, a ninety-eight-pound specimen of skin and bones from California's San Fernando Valley, began to accompany his mother on her rounds as a day worker cleaning homes in the affluent environs just beyond his lower-middle-class community of Roseda, California. Imbued with an urban moxie that seemed out of place in Roseda ("He'd never been to Brooklyn," said one acquaintance, "but he had a lot of Brooklyn in him") and driven by a childhood dream of becoming a millionaire before his twenty-first birthday, Minkow started a fledgling carpet-cleaning business, christening it "ZZZZ Best."

Displaying an intuitive gift for salesmanship and self-promotion, the high school sophomore quickly built his born-in-a-garage venture into a formidable enterprise boasting hundreds of employees and annual sales of more than $5 million. What had started out as a teenage version of the all-American lemonade stand turned in just a few years into a corporate meteorite pursued by the press, venture capitalists and investment bankers from New York to Los Angeles.

But true to the entrepreneurial spirit and to the big-buck psychology that set the tone of the decade, Minkow was far from satisfied with his precocious start-up. Although he had transformed himself from a California dreamer into a capitalist wunderkind, as far as Minkow was concerned, the world "ain't seen nothing yet." His goal was to create a new species of business, a carpet-cleaning giant ("the GM of the cleaning business"), and in the process to amass a personal fortune.

But to make the *Forbes* 400, Minkow knew he would have to stop cleaning carpets (where the profit potential was limited) and start using his promotional flair to sell a bill of goods to the financial community, which, in spite of its self-proclaimed sophistication, is forever turning con artists into superheros. With this in mind, Minkow decided to go public, and he soon established his company as the darling of Wall Street.

After merging his company into a publicly listed Utah shell corporation, Morningstar Investments, Inc., which enabled him to go public without a full-blown SEC registration, Minkow offered $13 million worth of stock to investors. For $12, each, they received units composed of three shares of common stock and a warrant entitling the holder to buy an additional share. The offering was attended to by prominent names in law and accounting. Serving as legal counsel was the New York law firm Hughes, Hubbard & Reed, and on the financial side Ernst & Whinney prepared a review report that was included with the prospectus. New Jersey–based CPA George Greenspan issued the certified statement for the public offering.

In promoting the ZZZZ Best offering to the public, Minkow boasted that his company had diversified into the lucrative insurance restoration business and that these restorations already accounted for 85 percent of ZZZZ Best's revenues. The way Minkow described it, ZZZZ Best would serve as a contractor to major insurance carriers, restoring homes and commercial establishments destroyed by floods, fires and other natural disasters. It was, the founder claimed, a burgeoning market his company was prepared to dominate.

To support this, ZZZZ Best's preliminary prospectus claimed that "the Company began its significant insurance restoration business in April 1985 and since then has performed restoration services for buildings ranging in size from 100,000 to 750,000 square feet. Restoration contracts, all of which are performed on a fixed price basis, have ranged from approximately $150,000 to $7,000,000. The Company has restored buildings located throughout California and in Arizona, with the majority being in Southern California. As of September 30, 1986, there were 13 insurance restoration projects in progress, under contracts aggregating $24,362,000 (including seven aggregating $15,068,000 through joint ventures), all of which are scheduled for completion within six months."

Touting the restoration venture as a runaway success, ZZZZ Best reported that its earnings had skyrocketed from $400,000 in 1983 to an estimated $40 million for 1987. During this period, the company's glowing numbers were reported in a hundred filings with the Securities and Exchange Commission and in quarterly financial statements.

With ZZZZ Best's sales curve looking like a Xerox-in-the-making, the company's stock soared from $4 to $18, propelling Minkow's personal wealth to more than $100 million. Quickly, he lavished upon himself a Ferrari and a luxury home in Woodland Hills, California. His ego soaring, the precocious entrepreneur, barely out of his teens, claimed there was no limit to the company's growth: ZZZZ Best, he promised, would be the financial juggernaut of the eighties.

This type of glowing projection was a key component of the Minkow formula. With every public announcement, he played to the greed, the get-rich-quick fantasy, the speculative fever that gripped Wall Street in the Reagan-era eighties. At a time when such corporate vultures as Henry Kravis, T. Boone Pickens and James Goldsmith were picking apart century-old corporations, and when a single lackluster earnings report would prompt institutions to bail out of a stock that had performed reliably for decades, Minkow knew instinctively that the darlings of the financial community were those who painted a tableau of dizzying growth, mind-boggling profits and meteoric stock prices. That's what he promised, and that's what the Ivy League, Hermes-clad "geniuses" on Wall Street believed.

Echoing Minkow's enthusiasm, Ladenburg, Thalmann & Company, a New York investment banking firm and a market maker in the stock, declared that "ZZZZ Best meets the criteria of a company that has the same potentially explosive sales and earnings characteristics and market opportunities that permitted McDonald's and 7-11 to reach the success each has achieved—sales of over $1 billion in a relatively short time from inception."

With ZZZZ Best being compared to McDonald's and Seven-Eleven, Minkow's company indeed seemed well on its way to becoming "the GM of the cleaning business." But it was all a hoax. The insurance restoration business that Minkow touted as the linchpin of his company existed on paper only. The fire-scorched buildings ZZZZ Best claimed to be restoring, the teams of workers allegedly restoring smoke-stained carpets, the reported contracts with the Allstates, the Liberty Mutuals and the Prudentials of the world were figments of Minkow's fertile imagination. In reality, the carpet-cleaning wizard had masterminded a complex Ponzi scheme, raising millions of dollars from unsuspecting lenders and investors only to shuffle the money among a series of dummy companies controlled by Minkow and his cohorts. As financial fraud specialist John Murphy later described it, ZZZZ Best was "a monstrous check kite. It was a cash racetrack."

Even more shocking than Minkow's gall in fabricating an entire business and thinking he could get away with it was the fact that he *did* get away with it—long enough to bilk ZZZZ Best investors of at least $70 million and to hoodwink one of the largest (and, by reputation, one of the finest) accounting firms in the world, Ernst & Whinney. The firm had been hired by ZZZZ Best in September 1986 to review the balance sheet and related financial statements as of July 1986, to assist in the preparation of the registration statement, to prepare a cold comfort letter, a document meant to assure the underwriters that the offering prospectus was basically accurate, and to audit financial statements as of April 30, 1987. E&W's total fee range was to be $41,000 to $72,500.

Just why Minkow chose to hire Ernst & Whinney at a critical stage in his company's life reveals much about the inner dynamics of the accounting profession and the business community at large. For years, investment bankers have demanded that companies availing themselves of the capital markets be audited by one of the accounting giants. This prerequisite created an oligopoly guaranteeing the accounting firms a hammerlock on all of the most prestigious and lucrative audit engagements. In spite of cases of sloppy and negligent work—some of which have resulted in massive and highly publicized audit failures—the financial community has continued to favor an audit by one of the "chosen firms." Aware of this, these firms have marketed their imprimatur like the Good Housekeeping Seal of Approval: "Work with us, and ye shall be blessed." It was with just such a blessing in mind that Minkow selected E&W to work with ZZZZ Best.

"Mr. Minkow came . . . to tell me that I had been replaced as the certifying accountant by Ernst & Whinney," recalled George Greenspan, ZZZZ Best's original CPA, in hearings before the House Subcommittee on Oversight and Investigations (January 27–February 1, 1988). "He was very sorry about this, but the underwriter and the banks required a Big Eight firm to take over the accounting, the auditing."

No one was more aware of the power of a big firm's audit signature than Minkow himself. With his phony company generating only a pittance in actual revenues, the smallest local CPA firm could have serviced him well. But it wasn't service the "boy wonder" was after; he wanted a credible image. So when ZZZZ Best went public, Minkow sought out E&W—and nothing could have pleased E&W more. With Minkow being hailed as a corporate phenom on the order of a Steve Jobs or a Saul Steinberg, he was the kind of dream client the big accounting firms were falling over themselves to attract. The way the thinking went was, if California's boy wonder thought highly enough of an accounting firm to select it as his auditor, other fast-track companies from Silicon Valley to Boston's high-tech corridor would get the message that these CPAs talked their language. With Minkow making the rounds on *Oprah Win-*

frey and the Los Angeles talk shows, E&W could brag, "That's our client, that's our boy," knowing that the publicity Minkow was garnering would rub off on them.

A born manipulator, Minkow instinctively recognized that accountants had tired of their image as the shlubs of the financial world. With this in mind, he hosted an extravagant bash celebrating ZZZZ Best's public offering. In a highlight of the ceremonies, Larry Gray—E&W's lead partner for the ZZZZ Best account—was called onto the stage to receive a trophy for E&W's role in the offering. While a traditional client might send its CPAs a thank-you note, Minkow presented his accountants with an "Oscar," and they adored him for it.

In light of his stature as an emerging superstar, Minkow wasn't as much a client as a trophy. Honored by the Association of Collegiate Entrepreneurs as one of the leading young business founders in the United States, he was a living embodiment of the great American success story. To E&W, keeping its grip on a prize of this magnitude had to be a high priority. For whatever reason—be it the stature of the client, Minkow's ability to snake-charm his CPAs, or the glamour of dealing with a "boy wonder"—E&W failed for some time to see through a company that was built on a foundation of fraud.

Consider the time E&W auditors decided to conduct a field inspection of ZZZZ Best's insurance restoration business, focusing on a particular work site in Sacramento, California. They called Minkow to schedule an appointment. Unfortunately for ZZZZ Best, which had dreamed up the restoration business, there were no work sites in Sacramento. But that didn't stop Minkow from complying with the request for a field inspection.

To do so, he set the wheels in motion for an extraordinary sting. Acting as an advance man, Mark Roddy—whose company, Assured Property Management, had been hired by ZZZZ Best to oversee renovation activities, traveled to Sacramento, where he took space in a furnished office suite made to look like Assured's local branch office. Operating from this base, Roddy identified a Sacramento office building that could serve as a stage for a mock restoration site. He then cut a deal with the building's security guard who, in return for a modest bribe, agreed to play a part in a charade in which, when the time came, he would pretend that he was familiar with ZZZZ Best's employees and knew about their role at the site.

Demanding that the examination be held on a Sunday, Minkow set the wheels in motion for the Sacramento flim-flam. On November 23, 1986, ZZZZ Best senior vice president Mark Morze squired Mark Moskowitz, a partner with ZZZZ Best's law firm, Hughes Hubbard & Reed, together with Ernst & Whinney's Larry Gray, to Mark Roddy's make-believe office in Sacramento. From there, the visiting "inspectors" were shepherded to the alleged construction site, where the security guard feigned familiarity with the ZZZZ Best representatives.

After a partial tour of the building, Larry Gray—who had been fed a cock-and-bull story about the causes of the interior damage—was sufficiently fooled by the Minkow sting to file this memo:

> We were informed that the damage occurred from the water storage on the roof of the building. The storage was for the sprinkler systems, but the water somehow was released in total, causing construction damage to floors 18 and 17, primarily in bathrooms which were directly under the water holding tower; then the water spread out and flooded floors 16 down through about 5 or 6, where it started to spread out even further and be held in pools.

We toured floor 17 briefly (it is currently occupied by a law firm), then visited floor 12 (which had a considerable amount of unoccupied space) and floor 7. Morze pointed out to us the carpet, painting, and clean up work, which had been ZZZZ Best's responsibility. We noted some work not done in some other areas (and in unoccupied tenant space). But per Mark, this was not ZZZZ Best's responsibility; rather it was work being undertaken by tenants for their own purposes.

In summing up, Gray noted, "ZZZZ Best's work is substantially complete and has passed final inspection." But in reality ZZZZ Best hadn't done a dollar's worth of restoration work. The leaks, the floods, the water damage— all were the components of an outrageous fraud that completely befuddled the auditors. Defending its failure to detect the truth, Ernst & Whinney later claimed that the Sacramento scheme was nearly impossible to uncover— but in fact the Los Angeles police department smoked it out with routine police work.

Consider this exchange between Rep. Ron Wyden and Mike Brambles (a detective with the organized-crime intelligence division of the Los Angeles Police Department) at the congressional hearings on the ZZZZ Best fiasco held in Washington on January 27 and February 1, 1988 by the House Subcommittee on Oversight and Investigations, which serves as the legislative branch's watchdog over the accounting profession.

Wyden: Did the building ever have any damage, or could they have found that out?

Brambles: The building did not sustain any fire or water damage. We ascertained that by checking with the building department of Sacramento in determining that in the previous two to three years there had been a very minor amount of construction work, that being only cosmetic in appearance and not involving fire and water restoration work.

Wyden: How long did it take your people to find out about the condition of the building?

Brambles: Approximately ten minutes at the building department and then roughly one or two hours at the restoration site.

Perhaps Ernst & Whinney failed to see through the ZZZZ Best fraud because the CPAs allowed Minkow to restrict their examination of his company's business activities. Claiming he had to protect the confidentiality of those involved in the restoration process (a suspicious request that in itself should have alerted the CPAs), Minkow convinced E&W to sign a "confidentiality letter" pledging that:

1. We will not disclose the location of such building, or any other information with respect to the project or the building to any third parties or to any other members or employees of our firm;

2. We will not make any follow-up telephone calls to any contractors, insurance companies, the building owner, or other individuals (other than suppliers whose names have been provided to this firm by the Company) involved in the restoration project.

That Ernst & Whinney would agree to have its arms tied behind its back in this way is shocking. If "independent" accountants consent to limitations on the scope of their examination, how worthwhile can that examination be? For its part, E&W would hold that it initially agreed to sign the confidentiality letters in reference to a review, not an audit. At that time, the firm says, it was clear in Larry Gray's mind that if he found irregularities, he would have to be allowed to pursue them or E&W would resign the engagement. The same thinking, E&W insisted, applied in reference to the audit work that would proceed (but would never be completed) after the review. But others saw no legitimate excuse for signing the letter. "We would never agree to a client's demand that we limit the scope of an audit," said Ted Levine, a senior partner and co-founder of the New York–based CPA firm of Richard A. Eisner & Company. "From our perspective, that would mean we couldn't do an effective or meaningful audit.

"Let's look at what happens when an auditor agrees not to make follow-up calls to companies involved in its client's business. Suppose the auditor sends out confirmation letters, asking these parties to verify receivables or other figures. Generally, these confirmation letters go to low-ranking employees, usually at the bookkeeper level. When questions arise, the auditors, who have agreed not to make follow-up calls, cannot gain access to high-level expertise and cannot resolve the questions they have.

"Auditors' duties are spelled out in volumes of technical literature. But you don't have to read them to understand, in principle, what we are supposed to do. We're supposed to demonstrate a 'healthy skepticism.' When a client asks an auditor to limit the scope of an audit, that skepticism should prompt the auditor to say, 'Wait a minute. Why do you want me to do that?' Anyone with any experience in this profession should know that whatever the client answers, something isn't right."

Just one sting on the magnitude of the Sacramento charade was mind-boggling. That experienced auditors could be so thoroughly duped raised questions about the competence of the premier auditing firms, on the faith the public should place in those firms and, in turn, on the checks and balances built into the financial system. But the ZZZZ Best scheme involved far more than one sting. Just three months later, Minkow and company arranged an encore presentation at a contrived site in San Diego. This time the Ernst & Whinney "inspection squad" was led to a newly constructed office building where ZZZZ Best had secretly leased 30,000 square feet of space for use as a mock restoration site. Once again, E&W had the wool pulled over its eyes.

Consider Larry Gray's memo on the visit:

We then visited the job site in San Diego—Fourth Street & Cedar—called Fourth Street Commercial Center. Mark Roddy of Assured met us there. This building was vacant. This is an eight-story building, plus a subterranean Executive Club (spa, handball, lockers, etc.) and three underground floors of parking. Per Morze the building is about four years old, and a fire on one floor spread to other floors through a faulty trash drop (where retaining doors had not been closed properly). Also, building had much water damage (particularly Executive Club) as the owner had delayed for about three days in selecting contractors—this caused even more damage.

We toured several floors and the Executive Club. It was a very clean job site. Insulation, replumbing of overhead sprinkler pipes, cleaning and repairing of all ducts was done. Building was ready for inspection on Monday. Following this, the wallboard was ready to go up (wallboard was on site), ceiling could be installed and carpet laid. It appears balance of work will go fast.

In the common area of each floor, painting was done, carpet down and basically this looked complete. However, Morze mentioned that they were going to take up carpet in common area and put down a padding. This was not required in the specifications, but the Company feels it is needed and will undertake to do this at no cost to the insurance company.

Here, as in the Sacramento "inspection," E&W had agreed to a "confidentiality letter," promising that:

> We will not disclose the location of, or any other information with respect to, the Project or the Warehouse, to any third parties or to any other members or employees of our Firm;
> We will not make any follow-up telephone calls to any contractors, insurance companies, the owner of the Project or of the Warehouse, or other individuals involved in the restoration project;
> We will not make any follow-up visits to the Project or the Warehouse, unless specifically authorized by the Company and Interstate Appraisal Services ("Interstate") [a company set up to appraise ZZZZ Best renovation projects].

When Congressman Wyden later questioned Gray about the confidentiality letters during the course of the congressional investigation, the E&W partner insisted they had done nothing to limit the firm's independence.

> Wyden: We go back to these confidentiality letters. They were signed by you personally, Mr. Gray, and they were signed also on behalf of Ernst and Whinney regarding the visits to phony insurance restoration jobs, one in Sacramento and San Diego. You mention personally in these letters on behalf of the firm that you won't disclose the location of the job sites to any third parties including other members and employees of the firm. You go on to proposals that you won't make any follow-up phone calls to any contractors, insurance companies, building owners, or other individuals involved in restoration projects.

I guess what raised my curiosity about these confidentiality letters is that I wonder how, after you signed them, you could then go out and independently verify material information given to you by ZZZZ Best management.

Gray: The signing of the letters does nothing to restrict what I wanted to perform. We—in fact it was done at the client's request. We get requests from our clients many times to confirm our confidentiality relationship. As I stated earlier, we have the overriding responsibility to keep our clients' information confidential. So them asking me to do this, my purpose was to go on the site and see the work done. It did not restrict me being able to perform that and I did go on site to see the work done, and Congressman, if I would have had any questions that came up in the course of that review, I would have pursued those questions and gotten answers to satisfy myself, or I would have quit.

Although Gray went on to claim that an extensive series of checks on the restoration project was made, the fact was that once again the Los Angeles Police Department quickly spotted what E&W had been unwilling or unable to discover.

Wyden: I just want to pin down that in San Diego, as at Sacramento, we had a situation where the building really didn't have any damage, and it wouldn't have been hard, as you said your own people could do, to determine that, is that correct?

Brambles: Yes sir, what we did was, we went again to the building department of San Diego and checked their construction permits on file. What our investigation determined was basically that the application for cosmetic construction had been applied for and granted by the city of San Diego. The permit was paid for, but it was never inspected by the building inspectors, it was never finalized.

That took us approximately ten minutes to do that.

We also checked to determine whether or not the building had received damage in the area of fire and water, and that turned up negative results as well.

Wyden: . . . what you have told us is that essentially in just a few minutes your own people could determine the job was a fake. But somehow the auditors didn't discover it, and it seems amazing . . ."

E&W didn't see it that way. Justifying its failure to do what the police had done, the firm held that it had had independent verification of the restoration contracts and at that point it had had no reason to doubt that ZZZZ Best had done the work as reported. "The government had something we didn't have," an E&W spokesman said. "They had the benefit of hindsight."

Just when it might be thought the absolute limit of corporate fraud had been reached, another layer of the ZZZZ Best scandal was peeled away, revealing even more shocking details. On another inspection in Dallas, Texas, E&W auditors, escorted by Mike Morze, were taken to a warehouse alleged to hold the supplies for a local restoration job. To create the impression of a busy facility, ZZZZ Best arranged for materials to be delivered to the warehouse at the time the CPAs were present. To reinforce the hoax, deliverymen were fitted out in uniforms bearing the ZZZZ Best logo.

Compounding the sting, the ZZZZ Best conspirators staged a fraudulent telephone conversation to coincide with E&W's visit. As Larry Gray's file memo on the inspection made abundantly clear, the auditors again took the bait:

During our visit, Mark Morze received a telephone call to advise that ZZZZ Best had just been selected to do two more buildings in the Dallas area. So they will have the current 4.9 and 2.8 million dollar jobs, plus a new 10.1 million dollar contract covering two more buildings. Morze advised that he will start immediately to secure more warehouse space close by, as they will need about twice the capacity to handle this new work.

Unlike the Sacramento and San Diego stings, where ZZZZ Best had arranged for mock restoration sites, in Dallas it used the address of a vacant lot (adjacent to a freeway on-ramp) and then dissuaded E&W from visiting the location. As Gray noted in his memo:

> Mark Morze, Dennis Harris and I visited Dallas following our San Diego stopover on May 11, 1987. We were going to visit the two contracts and the Warehouse, but I was informed that the contracts are in hard-hat stage and outside spectators were not allowed.

Had E&W insisted on visiting the Dallas restoration site, the ruse would have been uncovered. The question is, Why wasn't this done? Why would trained auditors accept the lame excuse that hard-hat work prohibited a visit? Why did they fail to challenge Morze's assertion that the site was unsafe? Was ZZZZ Best dealing with explosives? Could the building cave in on them? How dangerous could the place be? Restoration crews were allegedly on the scene. Why didn't E&W request a limited inspection of the site? Or even a cab ride past it? Had they done so, even master manipulator Minkow would have had a hard time turning a dusty vacant lot into a fire-damaged facility.

"Just having a client tell you not to visit a site should get the auditor wondering 'Why not?' said CPA Ted Levine. "If the place is too dangerous to walk around in, why not hire a professional inspector who can estimate the percentage of work that's been completed on the job? These are the kinds of things you do to verify that things really are the way a client says they are."

Were the E&W CPAs victims of the ZZZZ Best hoax (as they later claimed to be), or were they lax in their duties as public watchdogs? Although E&W denied any wrongdoing on its part, by willingly signing confidentiality agreements and in complying with ZZZZ Best's highly unusual demands, the firm appears to have accepted limitations that should have been taken as cause for great concern. There's no denying that E&W was the victim of a carefully planned scheme, but to knowledgeable observers a bit more in the way of "healthy skepticism" might have uncovered that scheme.

Traditionally, auditors have performed their work "by the book," following the required steps in their firm's audit manual and considering that to be the full extent of their obligation. Over the years, this base-covering has absolved those who went through the prescribed procedures whether the audit was successful or not. "Don't blame me," the excuse has always been. "I followed the rules."

When E&W's Larry Gray visited the Sacramento site, he appeared to be set on what he would review and what he would not review. He justified his actions in an exchange with Rep. Norman Lent at the congressional investigation.

Lent: And what did Ernst and Whinney do to verify the existence of the Sacramento job?

Gray: To verify the existence—let me just say I was going to Sacramento to review the site to support, help to support the revenues that ZZZZ Best was reporting from that site that affected the quarter that we were reviewing. So my purpose was to look at the percent completion and help gain an understanding of the work that had been performed at that site. That is why I went there.

Lent: In connection with that, did you check the building permit or the construction permit?

Gray: No, sir. That wouldn't be necessary to accomplish what I was setting out to accomplish.

Lent: And you did not check with the building's owners to see if an insurance claim had been filed?

Gray: Same answer. It wasn't necessary. I had seen the paperwork internally of our client, the support for a great amount of the detail. So I had no need to ask—to pursue that.

Lent: Had you done so, perhaps, might we have had a different result here?

Gray: I don't know. Again the fact remains I went there to accomplish a review objective, which I did accomplish.

Lent: That objective was not to verify the existence of the job?

Gray: Was to verify the work done to help support the revenues our client had recorded. So I saw evidence of the work done. I saw the work.

Lent: Like what?

Gray: I went throughout the building and saw evidence of the work, and the carpet, and the restoration work that had been accomplished. When I went there in late November the work and the contract under which ZZZZ Best was operating was about ninety percent complete and our client had been paid for the work that they had done. So it was substantially done when I went there in November.

Lent: You understand that what you saw was not anything that was real in any sense of the word?

Gray: I understand from what I read in the newspapers now, sir, and allegations I heard, Mr. Brambles, that there apparently were improprieties in that job, yes, sir.

Lent: And what you are saying is that if there was a fraud or someone was duped, that you were part of that? You are saying you were duped, are you not?

Gray: Absolutely. If what I read now are the facts, and I am not sure I know what all the facts are yet, but absolutely, it was a major sting.

At the time Ernst & Whinney was serving ZZZZ Best, auditors functioned under vague and fuzzy rules concerning the detection of fraud. The AICPA's Statement on Audit Standards 16 held that "within the inherent limitations of the auditing process," the auditor should "plan his examination to search for errors or irregularities [euphemisms for "fraud"] that would have a material effect on financial statements, and to exercise due skill and care in the conduct of that examination." In a subtle but profound distinction, auditors viewed their responsibility under SAS 16 as limited to planning the audit to search for fraud "within the limitations of the audit process," rather than being responsible for detecting fraud.

"As long as the auditors created an audit plan that they felt was designed to detect fraud, they felt they had met their professional responsibility," AICPA vice president Dan Guy explained. "Even if fraud was there and they failed to discover it, they were absolved as long as they had taken the search for fraud into account.

"For this reason, there was a tremendous gap between the public's perception of the auditor's role in detecting fraud and the auditor's perception of that responsibility. The former believed auditors were responsible for detecting fraud and the latter believed they were responsible only for designing an audit plan that recognized the possibility of fraud. Under the language of SAS 16, the auditors' responsibilities in the search for fraud were so loosely defined that they could justifiably claim that fraud detection was not one of their obligations."

Although SAS 16 seemed to have been written more to protect the auditor from legal liability (as long as he structured the audit plan properly, he covered himself in the event of fraud), it did state that "the auditor should plan and perform his examination with an attitude of professional skepticism." In at least part of E&W's work for ZZZZ Best, that attitude appeared to be missing. "Throughout the ZZZZ Best case it became clear to me that the auditors were taking at face value statements that cried out for further examination," Congressman Wyden said. "Something was clearly foul, but no one was getting to it."

Since the ZZZZ Best fiasco, a tighter auditing standard, SAS 53, has replaced SAS 16, putting the onus on the auditor to detect fraud by requiring that the audit be planned to provide for *reasonable assurance* of the detection of fraud. But even at the time E&W was serving ZZZZ Best, a long-standing industry practice was in place: In the event a client seeks to tamper with the scope of the audit, the auditor should at least disclaim the opinion, or perhaps even walk away from the engagement.

"When a client demands that an auditor sign confidentiality statements, that it not speak with or see certain suppliers, customers, documents or the like, that is unacceptable—period," said Dan Guy, referring to auditor responsibilities in general. "There are no ifs, ands or buts about it. There are more than audit techniques involved here. The client's demand that you refrain from doing something should raise the hairs on the back of your neck. And it should lead you to demand some very sound reasons why your activities should be limited. Failing to get that, the auditor's options are to withdraw from the engagement or to disclaim an opinion."

* * *

In the late spring of 1987, the incredible Minkow–ZZZZ Best story began to self-destruct. At the outset, only management insiders and their CPAs had any hint that something was amiss. Ernst & Whinney, then in the process of auditing ZZZZ Best's financial statements for the fiscal year ending April 30, 1987, was the first to get a clear indication that Minkow's "miracle" was being performed with mirrors. According to an investigation by the U.S. Attorney's Office for the Central District of California, "at least one individual informed Ernst & Whinney that one large job, a $7 million insurance restoration (purportedly in Sacramento on a commercial office building there) was a sham. . . . There was no job, no revenue, no profits."

The alleged informant, Norman Rothberg—who had visited the Sacramento restoration site as an employee of Interstate Appraisal Service—told E&W that the $7 million contract included in ZZZZ Best's financial statements for the quarter ending July 31, 1986, was phony, and furthermore that 80 percent of ZZZZ Best's income statement was incorrect.

Moving quickly to silence the informant and then to cover the trail of incriminating evidence, Minkow offered Rothberg $25,000 to recant his story. Soon after, Rothberg switched gears, telling the E&W auditors that he had been mistaken and that his previous charges should be ignored.

To licensed auditors—men and women trained to be professional skeptics—this "yes, they did it, no, they didn't do it" dog-and-pony show should have aroused great suspicion. Consider the implications: Was an E&W client engaged in fraudulent activity? Were investors being bilked for millions of dollars? Was a cover-up under way? Although E&W expressed concern to ZZZZ Best's board, it failed to communicate its suspicions promptly to law enforcement officials. E&W was not legally required to do so,* but Detective Brambles noted at the public hearings that prompt action on its part could have minimized losses resulting from the fraud: ". . . what occurred over a period of a few weeks was a series of meetings between Rothberg and Ernst & Whinney, at which time he then identified ZZZZ Best as the individual company perpetrating the alleged fraud in the Sacramento restoration site.

"That information was passed on to Barry Minkow, and then the bribe emanated from that. We feel that should Ernst & Whinney have advised either the Los Angeles Police Department or the federal investigative agencies involved in the investigation, the investigation could have proceeded somewhat more expeditiously and resulted in quicker results, possibly resulting in minimizing the loss to later joint-venture investors."

But in spite of the incriminating evidence from Rothberg and his later highly suspicious recantation, E&W apparently failed to revisit the site where the fraud was alleged to have taken place.

Lent: It came to your attention that Rothberg was talking about a certain company, namely ZZZZ Best?

Gray: Yes, sir. Yes, sir.

Lent: He was talking about fraud at ZZZZ Best and he mentioned that the Sacramento job was a phony job?

Gray: That is correct. We heard that on May 19.

Lent: You had been out there and you had walked that job, had you not?

Gray: That is correct, sir.

* Traditionally, CPAs have held that they are not obligated to be whistle-blowers and that assuming this role would impair the client communication that is essential to an audit. But Congressman Wyden is pushing for legislation that would require CPAs to inform regulators when illegal acts are detected during the course of an audit.

Lent: So you must have wondered whether you had been taken for a ride, whether you had been deceived, and it is logical to assume that you might have gone back there and looked at it over again, or made some further inquiry of the building department, the property owner, the contract, or other contractors, et cetera? You did none of those things?

Gray: No, sir.

E&W said that it had in fact acted on two fronts, launching its own investigations into ZZZZ Best and Rothberg and asking that the ZZZZ Best board conduct an independent investigation of the Rothberg allegations. In the meantime, the firm said, it held up additional work on the audit but did not resign from the engagement.

Still, Minkow's carefully planned fraud continued to unravel. A crippling blow came in the form of a May 22, 1987, *Los Angeles Times* story revealing that ZZZZ Best had filed false credit card charges. Quoted in the article, Minkow proclaimed ZZZZ Best's innocence in the scam, laying the blame on "unscrupulous carpet-cleaning subcontractors." Then he went a step further, issuing a press release to counter the suspicion generated by the *Times* story. ". . . ZZZZ Best is the victim," Minkow claimed. "The false credit card billings were submitted to ZZZZ Best by certain subcontractors who received a 50 percent commission on the gross amount submitted to ZZZZ Best.

"When the billings proved to be invalid, ZZZZ Best sustained 100 percent of the losses and immediately terminated the subcontractors involved. At no time did ZZZZ Best do anything improper . . ."

A week after the credit card story ran, Minkow tried to pick up where he had left off, issuing another in a long string of bold and optimistic reports on the company's financial performance. In a May 28 news release, ZZZZ Best announced record preliminary results for the fiscal year ended April 30 and a record level of new bookings. At this time, chairman Minkow trumpeted:

> The year-end preliminary results indicate revenues in excess of $50 million, earnings before taxes of $10 million, net income in excess of $5 million, and earnings per share of approximately $.50. This compares to fiscal 1986 results of revenues of $4.8 million, earnings before taxes of $1.8 million, net income of $900,000 and earnings per share of $.12.
> We have begun fiscal 1988 with record levels of business in each of our residential, commercial and restoration divisions. . . . Based upon our current annualized rate of new and repeat business, which is presently in excess of $100 million, we presently project substantial growth in revenues, net income and earnings per share for fiscal 1988.

But with the Rothberg allegations and the L.A. *Times* story, the smell of fraud was growing too strong to ignore. On June 1, 1987, Drexel Burnham Lambert resigned as ZZZZ Best's underwriter, pulling the plug on a scheduled private placement of debt securities to support Minkow's planned acquisition of the KeyServ Group, parent of Flagship Services, the national carpet-cleaning licensee for Sears, Roebuck. A day later, Ernst & Whinney ended its relationship with ZZZZ Best.

The change in auditors came about when CPA George Greenspan, then serving as ZZZZ Best's tax accountant, was waiting for E&W to complete its April 30, 1987, audit so that he could file the company's tax return. In his testimony at the congressional hearings, Greenspan said, "The treasurer of the company called me up and he said, 'We are in serious trouble. You cannot do your tax work because Ernst & Whinney refuses to certify the April 30, 1987, figures.'

"So he said, 'Do you have any association or any—could you refer us to another Big Eight firm?' I said indirectly I knew an accounting firm out in California where a lot of the partners came out of Price Waterhouse. So I called these fellows up, a very fine regional firm, and I said, 'Look, Ernst & Whinney resigned. I don't know why they resigned. I don't think there's anything wrong. Could you recommend a Big Eight firm? Maybe you can recommend a Big Eight firm whom you previously were employed by.

"They said, 'We'll call them up.' And before I knew it, Price Waterhouse was called in to continue the work of Ernst & Whinney."

With his company losing two of its prestigious outside representatives, Drexel and E&W, Minkow was in dire straits. The cover on his scheme was about to be blown. But the way the twenty-one-year-old con man saw it, this was just a modest setback. As he had done ever since creating ZZZZ Best, he would simply distort the truth, proving once again that he could manipulate the media, the stock market regulators and the Wall Street gurus.

On June 17, ZZZZ Best filed a mandatory 8-K document with the Securities and Exchange Commission, reporting a change of auditors and purporting to give the reason for the change. Signed by Minkow, the 8-K alleged:

Ernst & Whinney had been engaged to audit the Company's financial statements as of and for the fiscal year ending April 30, 1987, but resigned prior to completing such audit or rendering any report thereon. *There were no dis-*

agreements between the Company and Ernst & Whinney on any matter of accounting principles, financial statement disclosure or auditing scope or procedure, which disagreements if not resolved to the satisfaction of Ernst & Whinney would have caused that firm to make reference to the subject matter of the disagreement in connection with any report it would have prepared regarding the financial statements of the Company [author's italics].

Clearly, ZZZZ Best's 8-K filing created the impression of a routine auditor change from Ernst & Whinney to Price Waterhouse. With the big firms now declaring open season on one another's clients, and with clients regularly shopping the marketplace for lower fees, auditor changes were becoming commonplace among public companies. In this context, the announcement that Price Waterhouse was replacing Ernst & Whinney was hardly cause for alarm—just another case of the auditing musical chairs Washington and Wall Street were seeing with ever-increasing frequency.

But as ZZZZ Best knew full well, the 8-K was a misrepresentation of the facts. Contrary to Minkow's signed statement, the change of auditors was based, in part, on E&W's concerns over the validity of ZZZZ Best's financial statements—a concern that had begun with Rothberg's disclosures and that had grown geometrically as additional news came out. That Minkow would file a false and misleading 8-K is hardly surprising. But why Ernst & Whinney would fail to correct ZZZZ Best's statements for nearly a month was another matter. During that period of silence, investors failed to get the full picture about ZZZZ Best. Many must have assumed that the CPAs and, in turn, the SEC would blow the whistle if anything were really wrong.

* * *

Soon after ZZZZ Best filed its misleading 8-K report, the SEC, which had gotten wind of the Rothberg allegation, contacted E&W to learn whether it had the full story. That E&W would wait for the SEC to contact the firm, rather than taking the initiative on its own, infuriated Rep. John Dingell when he questioned both Larry Gray and Leroy Gardner, director of accounting and auditing for E&W's western region, during the congressional hearings.

Dingell: What happened to the stock during this period between June 2 and the date of bankruptcy on July 11? Did it go up or down?

Gardner: I didn't follow the stock.

Gray: It declined with the adverse publicity that was coming out.

Dingell: As a matter of fact, it lost about fifty percent of its value?

Gray: That may be the figure. I cannot recite the figures.

Dingell: The price per share on June 2, when you resigned, was around six or seven dollars. When the bankruptcy took place, which our colleague indicates was July 11, the stock fell to less than one dollar, something on the order of fifty to seventy-five cents; is that right?

Gray: I assume.

Dingell: I am wondering, is there some responsibility on the part of Ernst & Whinney to shareholders and other investors in this firm, or do you just have a peculiar special relationship with the firm?

Gardner: No, no. Our responsibility is to the public, to the investors.

Dingell: To the public and to the investors. How did you exercise that here? You initiated no contact with the SEC until July 16.

Gardner: No, no.

Dingell: Your contacts with the SEC on the seventeenth

and nineteenth were initiated by the SEC. You did not initiate that contact . . .

Gardner: I am sorry.

Dingell: The SEC initiated the contact with you on the seventeenth to the nineteenth. You were sitting tranquilly by, informing your former client, during that period of time?

Gardner: That is not correct, sir.

Dingell: Your first communication to the SEC was on July 18?

Gardner: After we talked with the SEC in early July, there was no point—

Dingell: They initiated that discussion; you did not?

Gardner: That is correct. We knew at that point what they knew.

Dingell: Happily they called you up. But your first communication to the SEC was on the sixteenth. If the SEC hadn't called you on the seventeenth or nineteenth, would you have called the SEC?

Gardner: Well, the fact is they did call us and they already knew the allegation.

Dingell: I know they called you. We are in agreement on that. That point is not in controversy. If they, however, had not called you on the seventeenth or nineteenth, would you have called them?

Gardner: I can't speculate about that.

"The failure to notify authorities about the fraud allegations is the kind of breakdown the current system permits," Congressman Wyden later said. "It should have put everyone on notice that something was amiss. The problem is, under current law auditors are not required to alert regulators regarding doubts and concerns they have about a client's representations. This violates the spirit of the auditor's role and leads to a wide gap between the CPA's view of [its] responsibilities and the public perception of those responsibilities." According to the complaint in a class-action suit filed by the San Diego–based law firm of Milberg, Weiss, Bershad, Specthrie, Lerach (on behalf of the purchasers of ZZZZ Best securities), ZZZZ Best lawyers at Hughes Hubbard & Reed threatened E&W with legal liability if it disclosed the Rothberg allegations, "and based on this threat, Ernst & Whinney had backed down and did not make or caused to be made any public disclosure of the true reasons for its resignation until after the end of the class period."*

Leroy Gardner recalled the confrontation with Hughes Hubbard & Reed this way: "Our firm, immediately after the resignation on June 2, immediately discussed with the company and its counsel, Hughes Hubbard firm . . . that we believed that the 8-K should contain a disclosure, that there was the allegation, disclose the facts of the allegation and the fact of the independent investigation . . .

"Hughes Hubbard's partner at the time disagreed with our position. They stated that the disclosure, if made, could cause serious damage to the corporation and they threatened our firm with financial responsibility in the event that disclosure upon the company by us . . . if it should later prove to be untrue. There were heated discussions during this period between top officials in our firm and Hughes Hubbard officials about that point. . . ."

Acting for E&W, the firm's in-house counsel, Douglas Galin, pressed Hughes Hubbard to include in the 8-K references that there were allegations of a phony contract and that the board of directors had launched an investigation

---

* The class period covered the time from the ZZZZ Best public offering to the day before the bankruptcy, when the Milberg, Weiss attorneys claimed that the price of the company's securities was artificially inflated.

into the charges. But the lawyers allegedly resisted on the grounds that Rothberg had recanted his charges and that until an independent investigation could be concluded, an announcement of allegations "would cause the stock to plummet to the damage of significant numbers of investors, because a premature or unbased allegation can have a detrimental effect."

This raised a disturbing question: By caving in to the Hughes Hubbard threat of legal action, was E&W putting its own interests before those of the investing public? Should an independent firm of certified public accountants, whose role is to serve as watchdogs of the public interest, allow what it believes to be an erroneous 8-K to go uncontested at the outset? Although E&W had no legal obligation to inform the SEC of its concerns, did it have an ethical responsibility to do so immediately? Clearly, one would think so, but E&W disagreed.

"We could not force ZZZZ Best to say what it didn't want to say in their 8-K," said an E&W attorney. "And Hughes Hubbard did have a valid point. If the board's independent investigation did not reveal any wrongdoing, raising these issues could bring unwarranted harm to the company. Similar thinking governed our response to the 8-K. If the allegations about ZZZZ Best proved untrue, there were no accounting disagreements between us. That's why we didn't respond immediately to the 8-K. We were hoping to learn more from the board's investigation before we responded."

As ZZZZ Best segued from E&W to Price Waterhouse, two new and disturbing factors came into play. PW claimed it had been given no reason why it shouldn't take on the ZZZZ Best engagement. In a June 3, 1987, memo recounting a meeting with E&W's Larry Gray, PW's Dan Lyle attributed these statements to Gray:

> Per Gray, E&W has no reportable disagreements to disclose in an SEC filing of the change in accountants. Further, there have been no significant disagreements on matters of accounting which are not yet resolved.
>
> Apparently, E&W has elected to resign, primarily because of concern as to the company's internal controls over long-term restoration contracts. . . .

In summing up, Lyle found little in the E&W interview to warrant rejecting the engagement.

> Other than the public information regarding bogus credit card charges and the audit difficulties E&W had experienced with the long-term contracts, Gray was aware of no matters we should consider prior to accepting the engagement.

Apparently E&W responded to Lyle's queries factually but narrowly. To each question there was a careful, studied answer that failed to explain any unresolved concerns E&W might have had. Looking back at the episode, PW people claimed that they were "pissed off" at "E&W's failure to tell us, 'Hey, guys, it looks like there's something ugly here.'"

But the fact was that PW hardly came away from the ZZZZ Best debacle looking like a paragon of professionalism. E&W did inform PW of the fraud allegations and the $25,000 payment offer related to them. From this alone, it might have seemed that PW should have recognized that it was walking into an audit minefield. Like its peers at the other big firms, PW touted its careful screening of prospective clients to weed out questionable engagements up front. But with ZZZZ Best, the screening procedures appeared to have lost their teeth. Just one of the conversations Lyle had with E&W should have been enough to keep prudent professionals at bay. In a June 4 memo, Lyle recalled:

> After a lengthy discussion, Gray noted, in passing, a $5,000 payment* E&W had noted to the individual who had made the allegations concerning the restoration contracts. Management had not informed E&W about any relationship with this individual. Gray had not followed up on the payment, had no idea as to its purpose, and no reason to doubt its appropriateness. The fact that the payment was made was a factor in E&W's decision to withdraw. *The matter will require immediate follow-up with Bruce Anderson, CFO.*

Question marks surrounding the ZZZZ Best audit were ominous enough to prompt Arthur Andersen and Coopers & Lybrand—both of which were asked to propose for the engagement—to back off after brief investigations. "When we visited ZZZZ Best for the purpose of conducting an initial audit scope, it became clear to us that the company's restoration activities were the largest part of the business," recalled Coopers & Lybrand partner Hal Schultz. "But when we asked to see certain documents, such as contracts for the restoration activities, they refused on the grounds that these documents had confidentiality clauses. For this reason, they informed us that the documents would not be available for the scoping or the audit. Based on this serious limitation, we felt we could not accept the engagement.

* (Representing part of the $25,000 offer)

The only time we would accept a confidentiality clause is if it had to do with national security."

This insight on the part of a peer firm made PW's willingness to accept the ZZZZ Best engagement all the more disturbing.

On June 18, ZZZZ Best made a public announcement that Price Waterhouse had replaced Ernst & Whinney as the company's auditor. At the time Minkow alleged that the resignation reflected "incorrect and/or misleading" news reports linking ZZZZ Best to the false credit card billings. Once again, the California wunderkind was practicing his own brand of damage control, stating that the resignation was in no way due to disagreements over accounting principles, financial statements or audit procedures. With an air of indignation, he announced that a special committee of independent board members would investigate the charges allegedly besmirching ZZZZ Best's good name and that the findings would be reviewed by a "major, highly respected law firm."

But the walls were collapsing, and even Minkow couldn't shore them up. From this point on, events moved quickly. On July 2, ZZZZ Best announced that Chairman Minkow had resigned for "severe medical reasons." Days later, the company admitted that there were significant questions concerning the accuracy of its financial statements and that it was under investigation by the SEC. On July 6, Hughes Hubbard did a 180-degree turn, resigning its representation of Minkow and filing suit against him for allegedly embezzling $18 million from ZZZZ Best. Less than twenty-four hours later, ZZZZ Best declared bankruptcy, followed shortly thereafter by Minkow's declaration of personal bankruptcy. With the company's false reports and pie-in-the-sky projections reduced to a stack of evidence in a fraud case, ZZZZ Best stock units, once as high as $66.25, plummeted to pennies. When the bankruptcy trustee sold the company's assets on July 24, 1987, "the GM of the cleaning business" fetched a paltry $62,000.

Only after the bottom fell out did Ernst & Whinney publicly refute the company's 8-K, acknowledging the reason it had resigned the ZZZZ Best engagement. In a letter to the SEC dated July 16, 1987, E&W stated that it had been engaged to perform an audit for the year ended April 30, 1987, but

> While we were performing our audit, allegations came to our attention (the principal one of which was that a major restoration contract of the registrant's was non-existent) which, if true, would raise issues as to the accuracy of the registrant's financial reporting and as to the integrity of some members of management. We reported those allegations to the management and the Board of Directors. At the time of our report on these matters to the Board we recommended that the Board initiate an investigation. . . . In addition, we communicated our concerns as to the problem with the registrant's internal controls, its accounting for restoration contracts and for the sales taxes on those contracts, and the registrant's transactions with entities that may have been related parties.
>
> Because the results of the investigation have not been made known to us and because we did not complete our audit, we are unable to state whether the allegations as to management were in fact accurate, or whether there ultimately would have been reportable disagreements as to accounting principles or practices, financial statement disclosure, or auditing scope or procedure. *However, overall, the information that came to our attention was of such a nature that we informed the registrant that we were re-*

signing because we did not want to be associated with its financial statements [author's italics].

After the filing of ZZZZ Best's false and misleading 8-K and Minkow's patently false statement that "there were no disagreements between the Company and Ernst & Whinney on any matter of accounting principles, financial statement disclosure or auditing scope or procedure" an entire month elapsed before E&W's letter to the SEC set the matter straight. "By the time that the response to the ZZZZ Best 8-K form was made by Ernst & Whinney, it was of no use to anyone, at least not to the investing public," said U.S. Attorney Robert Bonner at the congressional hearings. "The proverbial horse was already out of the barn."

Although E&W was within the letter of the law—which at the time required that auditors respond to client 8-K filings within thirty days—it had hardly acted as the watchdog the public expects CPAs to be. Referring to audit firms in general, Bonner noted:

The duties of an outside accounting firm, which is presented evidence which would lead a reasonable and prudent accounting firm to believe that fraud has been committed, that it is material, and that it has an impact on financial statements that have been previously filed and made public by the company, it seems to me rather elementary that accountants should have a duty that goes beyond informing management and resigning . . . at a minimum where an outside accountant learns such information . . . there ought to be some obligation to make a public disclosure of that information to appropriate authorities, such as a filing at the SEC by the accounting firm.

. . . you couldn't sell me on the idea that because management of the company is their client, they don't have obligations to the investing public; because that's precisely why independent auditors are there and are paid very handsomely to be there, to provide an independent objective audit of the company that the investing public can rely on.

Equally incensed, Congressman Dingell complained:

. . . we keep seeing this tremendous number of cases where supposedly men of goodwill are diligently watching and doing their job, but the public is being skinned, corporations are going under, rascals are prospering, honest men are suffering and the situation seems to be not improved. . . . We have this wonderful relationship that seems to exist between the accountants and the corporations.

The great irony in the ZZZZ Best case was that while the public and the investment community have long regarded auditors as the first line of defense against such corporate fraud and assorted book cooking, auditors have never viewed their role that way. "Before the Statement on Auditing Standards [SAS] 53 replaced SAS 16 in 1989, auditors assumed that their clients were honest unless evidence emerged to the contrary," said AICPA vice president Dan Guy. "In effect, they entered the engagement with a sense of trust, giving their client the benefit of the doubt."

Now, under SAS 53, auditors are supposed to take a neutral position, assuming at the outset that their client is neither honest nor dishonest. But acting on the earlier premise, the CPAs sent a clear message to the Barry Minkows of the world: Be exceptionally devious in your fraud, mount a major scheme to deceive us and you will likely succeed.

Judging by Mark Morze's comments to the Los Angeles Police Department, the ZZZZ Best conspirators recognized this weak link in the audit system: If care were taken to camouflage fraud, the CPAs were unlikely to detect it.

"Basically, the books would be tight and there was a good audit trail for everything," Morze said. "It's just that actual work wasn't being done. The verification of the work looked real good. There were voluminous data there to make it appear that what was being claimed was done. . . . People should dig deeper than most people do. A lot of people are more concerned about deniability than with the truth. If it looks like a duck and quacks like a duck, that is good enough."

Since the ZZZZ Best fiasco, new safeguards have been added to the audit reporting requirements. Due primarily to the Treadway Commission on Fraudulent Financial Reporting, new language in the auditor's opinion now includes this important reference: "We conducted our audit in accordance with accepted auditing standards. Those standards require that we plan and perform the audit to obtain reasonable assurance about whether the financial statements are free of material misstatement [another professional euphemism for "fraud"].

In part because of the ZZZZ Best scandal, changes were also made in the SEC reporting process. Now companies must file 8-K's within five business days (down from fifteen calendar days) after their auditors resign or are dismissed. In addition, the auditors must now file any response they have to the 8-K filing (specifically, the reason the engagement was terminated) within ten business days (down from thirty days). The idea behind both changes is to prevent the lengthy delay that may have led investors to believe all was well with ZZZZ Best when, in fact, management knew that the bottom was falling out.

But the question remains whether rules can assure investors, the business community and the general public of anything. Unless the Big Six view themselves as professionals, unless they place their watchdog role above the quest for growth and profitability, tighter reporting requirements will mean only that bad information is delivered faster. Should that be the case, the Minkows of the world will continue to evade detection long enough to fleece the unsuspecting of millions of dollars in investments—that the investors assume public auditors are there to protect.

In the end, the system caught up with Barry Minkow. In March 1989, the wayward Horatio Alger was sentenced to twenty-five years in prison and fined $26 million. Ernst & Whinney (now Ernst & Young) emerged unscathed. The firm denied any wrongdoing, basing its defense on the grounds that it never completed an audit of ZZZZ Best and thus never issued an opinion on the company's financial statements. Meanwhile, the class action suit filed against the firm by Millberg, Weiss is bogged down in judicial proceedings. Ultimately, the firm might be forced to pay heavy damages, but by January 1991 this was far from certain. Although E&W suffered through a spate of bad press reports resulting from the episode, it learned—much like the other accounting giants—how to ride out the nasty headlines until the news focus shifted to another incident, another firm.

2

WHEN TWO PLUS TWO EQUALS FIVE

The Strange Case of Touche Ross and
Beverly Hills Savings & Loan

They be blind leaders of the blind. And if the blind lead the blind,
both shall fall into the ditch.
—MATTHEW 15:14

The crisis in the savings and loan industry is without a doubt the gravest U.S. economic fiasco since the great stock market collapse of 1929.

By early 1991, more than five hundred troubled S&Ls had been seized by the federal government and others were teetering on the edge of extinction, producing widespread devastation throughout a critical sector of the financial system. For taxpayers, who will have to foot the bill for this debacle, the cost could mount to more than $200 billion.

But there is more than money at stake here. There is also faith—or lack of it—in the credibility of the independent audits that are supposed to serve as checks and balances on the S&Ls. In case after sordid case, insolvency after insolvency, S&Ls blessed with a clean audit opinion from the United States' premier public accounting firms have gone belly up only weeks or months after the auditors assured the world of their fiscal well-being.

How did this carnage in the thrift industry, long the rock-solid pillar of hometown finance, take place? Where did this once buttoned-down and thoroughly reliable industry go wrong? To find the answer, we must flash back to the early 1980s, when deregulation of the S&L industry freed the thrifts to depart from their traditional role as mortgage lenders. Overnight, a new era was launched. What had once been conservative institutions were now rushing pell-mell into a smorgasbord of sophisticated and often highly speculative financial transactions.

Just as the traditional practice of accounting changed dramatically in the 1980s, with the big firms moving head-long toward the Reaganomics ideals of power, prestige and the fast buck, so too did the deregulated S&L industry scale up its goals and expectations. Forced to pay rising interest rates to attract depositors, the S&Ls diversified their investment portfolios in search of higher returns, adding fly-by-night real estate deals and billions of dollars in junk bonds. With this change in direction, a once safe, prudent industry (like the once safe, prudent profession licensed to audit it) was suddenly charting new and un-known territory. Deregulation, a rallying cry of the Rea-ganites, had rewritten all the rules, changing what had been a highly structured marketplace for financial services into a free-for-all.

Testifying before the House Committee on Oversight and Investigation, partners from Coopers & Lybrand re-ferred to an

enormous convergence between once isolated sectors of the financial industry. Investment bankers and brokers are be-coming mortgage lenders and insurers, commercial bankers are becoming brokers, insurance companies are becoming investment advisers, investments in money market funds are comparable to demand deposits and thrift institutions are making commercial loans. This convergence gives the consumer the benefits of competition, but it imposes strain.

In this laissez-faire environment, the U.S. accounting establishment jumped on the S&L bandwagon, pursuing the thrifts as if they were Wall Street investment banks on the verge of the mergers and acquisitions boom. With the thrifts projecting enormous growth, CPAs sought to extend client relationships in the S&L industry, collecting fees they believed would mushroom over the years. But in the end, like the mergers-and-acquisitions boom itself, it all turned out to be a case of grand ambitions and spectacular busts. And as the S&Ls went down, they damaged the reputations of their auditors and subjected them to potentially devastating litigation.

In the raft of S&L audit failures that have tainted the accounting profession, two factors come into play. As the thrifts pursued more exotic investments, the time-honored techniques of auditing S&Ls were rendered obsolete. In effect, CPAs (most of whom had been trained in the old-school methods of S&L audits) were applying 1950s audit procedures to 1980s transactions. Add to this the competitive pressure to retain clients at any cost, and the stage was set for the scandalous specter of S&Ls being blessed by the CPAs only to become insolvent soon after.

"The horrendous problems we've seen in the S and L industry point up the fact that the Big Six have forgotten the social contract that gives them their license to opine on financial statements," said Spicer & Oppenheim's Steve

Oppenheim. "In return for this license, they are supposed to bring the highest levels of professionalism to their work. But the nonstop drive for growth, growth and more growth has interfered with that professionalism. When that happens—as the S and L fiasco proves so clearly—society is the big loser."

Although the Big Six now proclaim their innocence in the S&L crisis ("It wasn't our job to find fraud," they insist), a General Accounting Office study of eleven bankrupt thrifts revealed that the audits for six of the S&Ls failed "to meet professional standards." The firms involved included Arthur Young, Deloitte Haskins & Sells and Ernst & Whinney.

Central to the GAO's findings was the charge that the accounting profession failed to keep abreast of the fundamental changes sweeping through the thrift industry. As the GAO noted:

> The AICPA Audit and Accounting Guide for Savings and Loan Associations was last substantially revised in 1979.* It contains little discussion of the risks associated with land and ADC loans;† the effect of increases in restructured loans on collectibility; coordinating audit work with the results of regulatory examinations; the importance of disclosing regulatory actions and violations to depositors, shareholders, regulators and other users of audit reports. . . .
>
> A major portion of the S&L industry is in a financial crisis. It is important that CPA audits be performed in a quality manner to help the FHLBB [Federal Home Loan

* Revised standards are due in the summer of 1991.

† ADC loans are those for real estate acquisition, development and construction projects.

Bank Board] evaluate the condition of federally insured S&Ls and to help the FHLBB and others accurately gauge the extent and magnitude of the S&L industry's problems.

Although based on a limited review of 11 failed S&Ls, the results of our study indicate that significant improvements are needed in order to ensure that CPA audits of S&Ls are of adequate quality to permit the FHLBB and others to rely on CPA audits to determine whether S&Ls' financial statements are presented fairly and whether effective internal controls are in place. . . .

Lest anyone think that the failure of the CPA firms to perform in a professional manner was simply a case of audit complexity exceeding audit technique, the evidence indicates the contrary. In case after case, the CPAs failed to apply the most elementary aspects of professionalism to the audit process. Rather than acting in the legitimate capacity of trained skeptics licensed to serve as checks and balances on management assertions, all too often they simply rubber-stamped client statements, thus abrogating their duties as the public's watchdogs.

In hearings before the House Committee on Banking, Finance, and Urban Affairs, Frederick D. Wolf, the GAO's former assistant comptroller general for accounting and financial management, charged:

In many cases, management of troubled S&Ls contended that problem loans were collectible or, in cases of default, that collateral underlying the loans was sufficient to cover the outstanding loan balance. Standards require auditors to obtain independent corroboration that key management assertions are true—often a time-consuming but necessary audit function. However, the CPAs in our review did not always perform this function and, instead, often relied on management's unsubstantiated oral assertions that problem loans were collectible.

Citing another glaring lapse in the audit process, Wolf noted:

> Federally insured S&Ls are subject to examination by the Federal Home Loan Bank's auditors. These examinations are made primarily to help federal regulators know whether S&Ls are managed properly and whether they comply with federal regulations. They also provide useful information to a CPA who is issuing an opinion on the fairness of the financial statements. We identified cases where the auditor did not follow up on those problems which were identified by examiners and which we believe cast doubt on the S&Ls' financial statements.

This pervasive short-circuiting of the audit process was the inevitable fallout of a profession-turned-commercial-business. When a firm's primary goals switch from excellence to efficiency—and when the quest to retain clients and to maximize partner earnings supersedes all other objectives—the "time-consuming" steps of corroborating management assertions and following up on the red flags planted by federal regulators are often eliminated from the process.

The Big Six now claim they did not precipitate the S&L crisis, and they are right. But from all appearances, a shocking number of auditors at the premier CPA firms failed to honor their responsibility to inform the world of the deteriorating condition of much of the thrift industry. By playing deaf, dumb and blind, they allowed the industry's excesses to get out of hand. In the end, these excesses will cost American taxpayers hundreds of billions of dollars. Wolf revealed:

> In two cases in our review, CPAs did not point out in their audit reports that their S&L clients had materially misstated their income. In one of those cases, the S&L client had lost four times as much money as it had reported in its financial statements for that year.
>
> In some cases, CPAs did not report serious regulatory violations, such as excessive loans to single borrowers and formal cease-and-desist or similar orders by regulators. Thus, report users were unaware of those operating risks and the corresponding potential regulatory actions, all of which may have impacted the S&Ls' operations.

Bottom line: In a financial system based on the veracity of independent audits, a critical checkpoint failed. Given the Big Six's pervasive influence throughout the financial community, this dereliction of duty on their part has had a damaging influence on the federal government, the thrift industry and S&L investors and depositors.

"The S and L crisis is a textbook example of how the public's view of what auditors do, and what they really do, differs markedly," Rep. Ronald Wyden said. "The man on the streets doesn't want to know anything about generally accepted accounting principles. All he wants to know is how thrifts with clean audits can collapse so soon after those audits are completed. Oh, the accountants excuse this by saying they're not paid to be spies or policemen. But that's just an attempt to camouflage the issue. It didn't take policemen to see what was going on in these thrifts. The problems there were as big as the barn door.

"Given the fact that the financial markets were deregulated in recent years, the auditors were our last and, in some cases, our only line of defense. We needed them more than ever before, but unfortunately, in many cases they weren't there."

A list of government lawsuits (as of December 1990) against the giant accounting firms reveals the magnitude of the problem.

REVISED 12/03/90

ACCOUNTANT'S LIABILITY LAWSUITS
(Active Cases)

STATE	BANK	SUIT	DAMAGES (Approximate figures)
AR	FirstSouth, FA	*FDIC v. Deloitte Haskins & Sells and Touche Ross & Co.* LR-C-90-520 (USDC ED AR)	$400 million
CA	Beverly Hills S&LA	*FSLIC v. Dennis Fitzpatrick, et al.* (Touche Ross & Co.) CV 86-6780 (USDC CD CA)	$300 million
CA	Imperial Savings Association	*RTC as Conservator for Imperial Savings v. Ernst & Whinney* 90-0374-JLI (USDC SD CA)	$26 million
FL	Commonwealth FS&LA	*RTC as Conservator for Aspen SB Co. v. Deloitte Haskins & Sells, et al.* 89-6572-CIV-JCP (USDC SD FL)	$50 million

REVISED 12/03/90
ACCOUNTANT'S LIABILITY LAWSUITS *(cont.)*
(Active Cases)

STATE	BANK	SUIT	DAMAGES *(Approximate figures)*
FL	Duvall FS&LA	*RTC as Conservator for Duvall FS&LA v. Peat Marwick* 89-085-48 CA (4th Jud. Cir. Ct.)	$16.6 million
FL	Royal Palm FS&L	*RTC as Conservator for Royal Palm FS&L v. Deloitte Haskins & Sells* 89-8039-CIV-Paine (USDC SD FL)	Amount undetermined
OK	Peoples Federal	*RTC as Conservator for People's Federal v. Touche Ross & Co., et al.* 90-C-221-B (USDC WD OK)	$467,000
TN	City & County Bank of Anderson	*FDIC v. Ernst & Whinney* CIV-3-87-364 (USDC ED TN)	$255 million (for the following [4] TN cases)
TN	City & County Bank of Knox County	*FDIC v. Ernst & Whinney* CIV 3-87-364 (USDC ED TN)	
TN	First Peoples Bank of Washington County	*FDIC v. Ernst & Whinney* CIV-3-87-364 (USDC ED TN)	

71

REVISED 12/03/90

ACCOUNTANT'S LIABILITY LAWSUITS *(cont.)*
(Active Cases)

STATE	BANK	SUIT	DAMAGES *(Approximate figures)*
TN	United American Bank in Knoxville	*FDIC v. Ernst & Whinney* CIV 3-87-364 (USDC ED TN)	
TX	Western Savings Association	*FDIC v. Ernst & Young and Arthur Young & Co.* CA-3-90-0490-H (USDC ND TX)	$560 million

As the full extent of the S&L crisis began to emerge, and as the auditors' role in the debacle came into sharper focus, government actions against the big accounting firms intensified. By early 1989, the Federal Home Loan Bank Board had suits pending against a number of auditors, including the future merger partners Deloitte Haskins & Sells and Touche Ross. In many ways, the Touche Ross case—involving the audit of Beverly Hills Savings & Loan (BHSL)—reflected in microcosm the reckless practices of the thrift industry and the alleged role of the big accounting firms in the emergence of this national scandal.

The roots of the episode date back a half century to the founding of Beverly Hills Savings & Loan as a federal savings-and-loan association. For the first forty-four years of its existence, the thrift operated in the tried-and-true S&L format, taking deposits and using the proceeds to make standard mortgage loans. It was a reliable, steady-as-you-go business.

All of which changed abruptly in 1980, when BHSL,

which in 1979 had converted to a state-chartered association, embarked on a two-pronged campaign to achieve rapid growth. First, the thrift pursued jumbo deposits from stockbrokerage firms, using the carrot of high interest rates to lure money into its coffers. This part of the strategy worked exceptionally well. From 1980 to 1984, BHSL's deposits soared from $290 million to $2.3 billion. Second, BHSL launched into a series of aggressive investments—including stakes in real estate development companies, construction loans and junk bonds—that promised to generate higher yields than the old bread-and-butter mortgages. This was done to pay the high interest rates that had lured the massive inflow of deposits into the thrift in the first place.

Behind the scenes, BHSL's CEO Dennis Fitzpatrick—a University of California at Berkeley graduate with degrees in aerospace science and business administration—concocted a master plan for transforming the thrift from a sleepy S&L into an aggressive financial institution capable of competing in the new deregulated environment. At hearings before the House Subcommittee on Oversight and Investigation, held in the summer of 1985 to investigate the BHSL matter, Fitzpatrick made the following statement:

> . . . it became apparent to me and to the management team at Beverly Hills Savings that we could no longer allow ourselves to be subject to the vagueness of the money market; we could not survive if we continued to do business in the traditional fashion. Unless we responded innovatively to the emerging realities of the savings and loan business, we were doomed. In the face of the crisis, our management team developed a five-year plan which we initiated in late 1982.

The plan featured five major components:

- BHSL would raise funds on a wholesale basis rather than through the retail branch structure, which would bring much larger deposits into the thrift.
- BHSL would become a full-service real estate–financing concern. This move was based on an underlying conviction that Southern California would become an increasingly important factor in the national and international economy. According to Fitzpatrick, the goal of becoming a major force in real estate financing would be accomplished by "generating a large volume of single-family residential loans to homeowners; placing approximately ten percent of our assets in construction loans; originating permanent loans on commercial properties; placing approximately seven percent of our assets in real estate joint ventures; and acquiring real estate for sale in syndication."
- BHSL would develop a "matched book." By this it meant it had devised a method for raising capital that it believed would enable it to gather deposits "that could be matched with our loan and investment assets, both in terms of positive yield spreads and in matching maturities."
- BHSL would strive for growth. The idea here was to make the thrift's old, low-yielding loan portfolio a smaller percentage of total assets. And, Fitzpatrick said, this "would provide us with the opportunity to develop the 'matched book' goal and to establish and maintain that position."
- BHSL would generate higher fees to offset the lower spreads it would have to work with.

Beverly Hill's management team saw this master plan as a blueprint for success in a highly competitive decade. But smack in the middle of the plan, a power struggle developed, pitting businessman/investor Paul Amir against the Fitzpatrick-led management team. A transplanted Israeli who moved to Los Angeles in 1960 and became one of the city's most prolific real estate developers, Amir launched a takeover move in 1983. Acquiring 14.5 percent of the thrift's outstanding shares, he announced plans to gain control of the fast-growing S&L and in the process to oust the Fitzpatrick management team.

Determined to thwart Amir and retain control of the thrift, the BHSL board entered into a white-knight agreement with a group headed by Swiss entrepreneur Werner K. Rey that enabled the group to acquire 330,000 shares of Beverly Hills stock plus a $20 million debenture convertible into 833,000 additional shares. At the same time, BHSL purchased a series of Rey-controlled properties and assumed a share of his liabilities for a total of $33 million. Through this give-and-take process, BHSL effectively financed Rey's stock purchases. According to the FSLIC, these purchases gave Rey and his associates control of the thrift.

As part of the white-knight agreement, Rey and his affiliated companies commenced a series of transactions with BHSL, selling the thrift a real estate portfolio that included:

- Real property located in a Stockton, California, industrial park
- Fifty percent of the capital stock of Adamuz N.V., a Netherlands Antilles corporation that owned commercial real estate interests
- Ninety-eight percent of the capital stock of 59th Street Venture Corporation, which owed a stake in a New York office building
- All of the capital stock of Dilroad N.V., a Netherlands

Antilles corporation that owned an office building in Charlotte, North Carolina
• A 25 percent interest in San Diego's Intercontinental Hotel

Referring to the San Diego investment, BHSL's 10-K for fiscal year 1983 noted that "the Association has developed the expertise among its employees and its contacts within the real estate investment community to enable it to structure large, one of a kind transactions with complex financing arrangements . . ."

That would seem to have been an understatement. From the beginning, many of BHSL's real estate transactions were embroiled in controversy. For example, charges were made that it had overpaid for many of the properties it invested in. Consider the case of the purchase of Swan Run, a Charlotte, North Carolina, apartment complex BHSL acquired from the Werner Rey group. BHSL assigned Swan Run a book value of $3.1 million, but an independent report prepared three months after the purchase painted a picture of a nearly worthless tenement:

> With the exception of three buildings, the property has not been painted in some time, the gutters are falling down, the downspouts are off, porches have little or no screens, there is rotten wood, windows are broken, front doors are peeling, the landscaping is almost nonexistent, pavement is broken up, and large areas are not paved at all.
>
> Very large dogs roam the grounds, residents work on cars on Saturday and Sunday in the parking lots, motorcycles, bikes and neglected wood piles abound in breezeways, on patios, and on walks. Basketball goals sag, the word "pot" was spray-painted in white on the end of a two-story brick building. The laundry room, which was just

completed six months ago, was filthy and looked about six years old. The pool area is scraggly, a cover on the pool has two feet of water on it. There is no pool furniture.

An apartment was filled with sewage, under almost all of the buildings there is between three to fourteen inches of water, appliances are missing from almost all vacant units, all carpets need to be replaced, all appliances, if they are there, are in bad, if not inoperable condition, and should be replaced. This includes stoves, dishwashers, refrigerators, disposals, and traps.

BHSL's $800,000 purchase of the Tyron Tower Building, also in Charlotte, appeared to be another horrendous investment. As it turned out, the building had been gutted by a previous owner, which had left it with such little support that it was considered structurally unsound. In fact, an exception on the title report indicated that the city would not let the property be occupied until it was brought up to code. Soon after BHSL purchased the property for $800,000, its value was appraised at about half that sum. Adding insult to injury, the building's future earnings potential appeared to be nil.

Still, the battle for control of BHSL continued in spite of the thrift's real estate boondoggles. When Werner Rey's attempted white-knight takeover came up short, Paul Amir stepped back into the fray, turning up the pressure to oust the Fitzpatrick team. At this point, a new white knight, New Jersey–based Triangle Industries, emerged as a potential acquirer of BHSL. In February 1984, Triangle offered $109 million ($30 a share) for the thrift.

In a deal worked out between the opposing factions, Triangle then agreed to raise its bid to $32 a share in return for support by Amir, whose holdings had grown to 17 percent of BHSL's outstanding shares. But just as it appeared that a deal was in the offing and that the battle for BHSL was over, Triangle got cold feet and in April it called off its bid. With that, BHSL stock, until then buoyed up by the appearance of extraordinary growth (assets had soared from $820 million in 1982 to nearly $3 billion in 1984) and by expectations of a rich takeover, plummeted from a high of over $26 to $13.25.

After this, events moved quickly. As part of his negotiations with BHSL's board concerning the Triangle bid, Amir hammered out an agreement stipulating that he would be elected CEO in the event that the deal unraveled. Thus on April 11, 1984, two days after Triangle withdrew its takeover bid, Amir was installed as the thrift's chief executive and vice chairman. Although the initial announcement stated that Fitzpatrick would stay on as president and a member of the board, his position was filled in June by Michael Flaherty, a lawyer and thrift executive—and at the time president of the Southern California Savings and Loan Association—who assumed the roles of president and CEO. Amir then took the title of chairman.

But despite the change in management, BHSL's losing ways were coming home to roost. Citing "questionable" real estate loans, BHSL reported a 1984 third-quarter loss of $10.1 million (compared to earnings of $548,000 in the third quarter of 1983). But that was only a hint of the devastation to come. In April 1985, the thrift announced a delay in the completion of its audit for 1984 but indicated that the S&L might record a loss of approximately $100 million and that this could result in a negative net worth of $65 million based on generally accepted accounting principles. BHSL's shares, which had been on a rollercoaster ride during the on-again, off-again takeover period, slumped to $3.25.

*   *   *

As it turned out, the "miracle instrument" of the decade (the junk bond) and the "miracle firm" behind it (Drexel Burnham Lambert) played a role in the thrift's declining fortunes. With BHSL struggling mightily to meet its obligations between March and December 1984, BHSL's junk bond portfolio grew to more than $300 million, which represented over 10 percent of the thrift's assets. In April of that year, a junk bond salesman from Drexel's powerhouse Beverly Hills office (home of junk bond czar Michael Milken) recommended that the thrift buy into the junk bond issue of a company called Cell Products.

According to a suit later filed by BHSL against Drexel Burnham Lambert, the salesman pitched the Cell bond, touting the company as a solid, rapidly growing manufacturer and stating that the note would be secured by a deed on Cell's factory. On this basis, BHSL invested $3.69 million in the junk issue. But soon after, the bond went bad, leaving the thrift with nothing to show for its investment. When a BHSL contingent went to question Milken about the bond, it witnessed firsthand the arrogance of the junk bond king. As Amir recalled, "He treated us like a nuisance. What's three million dollars to him?"

And where were the public's watchdogs while all this was going on? Let's take a closer look. Federally insured S&Ls must undergo annual audits by independent accountants. The auditors' opinions can range from "unqualified" (meaning that the company's financial statements are fairly presented in accordance with generally accepted accounting principles [GAAP]) to "qualified" (financial statements are presented in accordance with GAAP except for an identified problem) to "adverse" (meaning the financial statements are materially misstated and are not fairly presented in accordance with GAAP) to a "disclaimer" (the company's internal records and controls are so haphazard that the accountants cannot fairly audit its financial condition, or the scope has been so restricted by the client that an audit cannot be performed).

When an S&L is blessed with an "unqualified" opinion complete with the prestigious signature of a prominent CPA firm, the public rests assured that it can take comfort in its financial statements. But according to the complaint in a lawsuit filed by the FSLIC, that wasn't the case with BHSL's auditor, Touche Ross.

> . . . Touche rendered its written opinion that Beverly Hills Savings & Loan's consolidated financial statements "present fairly the consolidated financial position of Beverly Hills Savings and Loan Association and subsidiaries . . . in conformity with generally accepted accounting principles applied on a consistent basis." At the same time Touche rendered these written opinions, it knew or should have known that such opinions were materially false, inaccurate and misleading in that BHSL's consolidated financial statements as of December 31, 1982 and 1983 did not present fairly the consolidated financial position of BHSL and subsidiaries as of those dates. . . .

For its performance on the BHSL engagement, the FSLIC sued Touche (the FDIC is now conducting the suit) for a laundry list of violations, including "breach of written and oral contracts, breach of implied covenants, breach of fiduciary duty, professional negligence and negligent misrepresentations." The significance of this and similar actions against major CPA firms is clear: When the auditor's signature is based on a questionable audit, faith in the system is threatened. Like a house of cards, it can easily collapse.

A closer look reveals what Touche Ross could or could not have done in its position as BHSL's auditors. A critical component of the government's case centered around the so-called Stout Apartment Program. Beginning in 1982 and continuing through 1984, BHSL, along with real estate entrepreneur James D. Stout, a Southern California phenom whose 1984 earnings were reported to be $6 million, invested in approximately fifty-six apartment projects. In an interview with *Money* magazine, Stout boasted that his favorite "toys" included a $5 million house on Harbor Island off Newport Beach, a Rolls-Royce Corniche, a Cadillac limousine and a Learjet.

The way the Stout/BHSL joint venture was structured, Stout found the apartments for investment and BHSL put up the money to buy them. In return for its investment, the thrift was entitled to 60 percent of the anticipated appreciation on the properties. With the California real estate market still bubbling merrily at the time, the thrift's management assumed that these investments would appreciate substantially and net a high return for the S&L, which by that point was on the fast track seeking quick growth in its assets and profitability. But according to the government, BHSL's quest for megagrowth "committed [it] to large-scale financing of activities such as acquisition of real estate; acquisition, development and construction lending; loans on commercial and industrial properties and investments in speculative securities, all of which involved excessive risks."

Clearly, the risk inherent in the Stout Apartment Program was that the properties would fail to appreciate to the extent that management had projected or, worse yet, that the apartments would depreciate, jeopardizing BHSL's investment.

"BHSL's idea was to work the properties free of the rent controls imposed on them by the Housing and Urban Development Corporation, which had subsidized their development," said Ann Buxton Sobol, associate general counsel of the FHLBB at the time the Touche suit was filed and now assistant general counsel for the FDIC. "Had this been accomplished, rents could be raised, the income stream increased and, as BHSL planned it, the apartments could be sold for substantial profits.

"As part of this strategy, BHSL talked—at different times—about syndicating the buildings or selling them to foreign investors. But these transactions never worked out. Attribute that, in part, to the nature of HUD properties, which have limitations on how they can be bought, sold and owned."

To complicate matters, the California real estate market turned sour, abruptly ending the long period of double-digit appreciation and putting the kabosh on BHSL's plans to sell the Stout apartments for a tidy profit. According to the government, this prompted an unscrupulous change in the way the apartments were accounted for. As Sobol put it:

"In the beginning, when BHSL believed that it would record hefty gains on the Stout sales, the thrift recorded the apartment acquisitions as investments," Sobol said. "But when it became clear in the spring of 1983 that there would be difficulty in selling the properties, and that the S and L would have to record losses from carrying them, they decided to stem those losses by changing the book-keeping of the apartment acquisitions from investments to equity participation loans, with the Stout entities as the borrower."

That change had a major impact on the thrift's financial reporting. When an S&L treats its participation in real estate projects as loans, interest and fees can be recognized as income as these sums accrue, even if no cash is received until the properties are sold. But if the thrift treats its participation in the same deals as investments, income cannot be recognized until payment is actually received.

"As the deals were restructured, Beverly Hills' share of the equity in the properties declined on the face of the transactions from sixty percent to forty-nine percent," Sobol said. "This was designed to further the appearance that these were loans as opposed to investments. Under the restructuring, BHSL also was to receive a commission on the sale of properties of three percent of the gross sales price, which had the practical effect of maintaining Beverly Hills' recovery on the sale at about sixty percent of equity.

"But it was all form over substance. No matter what they were called, these transactions were still investments. BHSL put in all the cash, the 'borrower' put in no cash; BHSL stood to recover more than fifty percent of the upside; and BHSL had all the risk of loss."

It is on the critical loan-versus-investment issue that the government is resting its case against the CPAs. "Touche Ross's culpability in this," Sobol charged, "is that it approved the treatment of BHSL's participation as loans, even though guidelines issued by the AICPA indicated that real estate ventures like the Stout program should be treated as investments."

Questioned about the transformation of equity investments to loans, Touche's former engagement partner for BHSL, Nelson Gibbs, concurred that Touche had advised the thrift that it could treat the Stout deals as loans. But in seeking to support the firm's actions in public hearings before Congressman Dingell's subcommittee, the Touche partner won hardly any converts in Congress.

Dingell: On what grounds could they be accounted for as loans?

Gibbs: Based on the contractual relationship between the parties and the equity in the interest.

Dingell: What was the equity at this particular time?

Gibbs: The amount of the equity?

Dingell: Yes.

Gibbs: I don't know.

Dingell: Was there any equity?

Gibbs: I believe there was, yes.

Dingell: You believe, or you know?

Gibbs: I believe there was. I don't know the amount.

Dingell: You don't know? You don't know the amount? You believe. Now, when one believes, one believes without knowledge. I believe in the Holy Trinity. I do not understand them. I have never seen them. I do not know what they look like. I do not know how they function together. But I believe in them. But I do not know. I believe.

But I know that you are sitting there at the witness table. That is knowledge. You understand the difference?

Touche argued that the Stout acquisitions were not subject to the AICPA's rules on ADC loans because these were existing properties with existing cash flows (which is not typical with ADC loans) and (also atypical of ADC loans) there was a cross-collateralization agreement between Stout and BHSL (meaning, according to Touche, that the lender had recourse to assets outside the project). Under the cross-collateralization agreement, BHSL could claim whatever equity it had in other projects with Stout, should any of the investments go bad. Lawyers for Touche Ross also claimed that "the Stout Apartment Program did not involve new construction and therefore the loans were not acquisition, development and construction loans. The accounting principles concerning ADC loans were developing in 1983 and 1984 and continue to evolve today."

But according to Sobol, Touche's argument that cross-collateralization changed the economics of transactions sufficiently to warrant the change from investment to loan accounting was unfounded: "BHSL didn't really get anything through the cross-collateralization on the loans that it didn't already have when the deals were structured as investments. The investment transactions included a provision for preferred return for BHSL that was the functional equivalent of interest. Stout and his associates guaranteed that BHSL would receive its preferred return, and their guarantee was collateralized not only by real estate including Stout's home, but also by their equity interest in the apartment buildings. In this sense, under the investment approach, BHSL's return on the program as a whole was collateralized by the equity in the projects. Similarly, under the loan program, repayment of BHSL's loans was supposedly cross-collateralized by the equity in the properties.

"Moreover, whether you are talking about investment or loan accounting, cross-collateralization is meaningful only if there is in fact equity in the properties. Touche's auditing on this point was inadequate—they relied on deficient valuations of the properties, and they relied unreasonably on BHSL's puffed-up values. They did not have sufficient evidence to support a conclusion that the properties were worth enough to cover the debt senior to BHSL and BHSL's loans."

* * *

The government's suit against Touche Ross has yet to come to court, and thus there is no judicial determination as to who is right about the accounting issue. But by early 1991 the parties were apparently reaching a settlement whereby Touche would pay an undisclosed sum of money without admitting or denying guilt. Touche's justification for its actions regarding BHSL may be accurate. Certainly, it is predictable. When CPA firms opine on accounting issues, they declare that their opinions are based on a bedrock of technical rules and guidelines. Although this is true in most cases, what the firms fail to admit is that another factor, competition for clients, can figure into their decision making.

Interestingly, competitive jockeying was going on behind the scenes of the Touche/BHSL relationship. As Touche was grappling with the issue of how to treat BHSL's plan to switch from investment to loan accounting, word reached the firm that Arthur Andersen, which had done work for Stout, had taken a liberal view of similar transactions. Although Andersen never took an official position on BHSL's plan to treat the Stout participation as loans, Stout executives kept Andersen partners up to date on the deliberations going on at Beverly Hills. Sensing that there might be a falling-out between Touche and BHSL over this issue, Andersen believed there was a strong opportunity to win the engagement.

In a memo dated March 25, 1983, between Andersen partners in the firm's Orange County and Los Angeles offices, mention was made of a contact who informed Andersen "that Touche Ross is clearly going to be replaced this year, and we have an excellent opportunity to be appointed as auditors." In addition, a letter from an Andersen partner to a Stout executive stated the partner's thoughts on a hypothetical S&L real estate investment by saying that "in our opinion, under generally accepted accounting principles, the transaction could be accounted for as a loan and not as an investment in real estate."

Although the Andersen statement was not an official opinion of the firm, was not made to BHSL and did not relate specifically to the terms of the BHSL transaction, word of Andersen's thinking even in the broadest terms had to worry Touche. As all accounting firms are well aware, clients determined to have their way on critical issues will often shop for the "right" audit opinion, using the competition among the firms to find a "cooperative" auditor. Those that fail to cooperate often lose the business.

Andersen partners referred to this unfortunate fact of life in an interoffice memo, noting that "Peat Marwick had taken a hard line on this issue and recently lost the Broadview Savings & Loan account because of its position." The memo went on to express various concerns about treating the BHSL transactions as loans, but then said that "we certainly would be willing to listen to the management of Beverly Hills Savings & Loan and confirm and get additional facts. . . . The decision as to the proper accounting, after considering all of the relevant facts, would be up to the audit engagement partner, the office managing partner and our office audit practice director." But a meeting between BHSL and Andersen never took place.

Meanwhile, at Touche, the question of how to treat the BHSL transaction moved up from the firm's local client office to that of one of its technical gurus, Robert Kay, who in turn called Arthur Wyatt, his peer at Andersen's Chicago-based accounting principles group. Referring to a May 1983 telephone conversation, Wyatt recalled that "Kay told me that his firm was confronting an ADC loan-accounting issue with BHSL and had been told by its client that Andersen had a more liberal view of ADC transactions than Touche. He said he would like to discuss my current approach to ADC transactions and I agreed to share my thoughts with Mr. Kay."

After speaking with several of his California partners, Wyatt conferred with Kay and a number of Touche Ross accountants. When the Touche people described the Stout arrangements, including BHSL's original 60 percent equity kicker in the deals, Wyatt stated his opinion "that a transaction in which the lender retained an equity interest greater than 50 percent should be recorded as an investment and not as a loan." Although Wyatt said that he "would consider accepting loan treatment if the equity kicker was reduced below the 50 percent threshold [as would happen in BHSL's restructuring]," he insisted that "it was necessary to understand and evaluate all the facts of each individual case."

Andersen's comments hardly qualified as an official opinion. But in an interoffice memo dated August 3, 1983, concerning "the issue of when a transaction is classified as a loan versus when it constitutes an equity investment," Kay noted that Touche had been pressed by a client to review "the matter with Arthur Andersen, who was alleged to have a more moderate view. We did this, on May 11, determining that Andersen's position at the time basically was arbitrary—if the lender had an equity kicker under 50 percent, it could be treated as a loan."

But according to a lawyer for Touche Ross, the firm "did not ask for Arthur Andersen's opinion on Beverly Hills' accounting." Instead, he said, "Touche Ross weighed the information it obtained from Arthur Andersen along with the available professional literature and current practice in coming to its own conclusion that Beverly Hills' choice of loan accounting was appropriate."

At least one Andersen partner believed that his firm's views influenced Touche Ross to accept the loan treatment. In an interoffice memo dated December 1983, he noted that "apparently based on our views, Touche Ross changed their views and allowed the savings and loan to account for certain transactions as loans as opposed to investment in joint ventures."

In a third-party complaint filed against Arthur Andersen, BHSL officers and directors charged that Andersen did, in fact, concur with Touche's treatment of the transactions as loans. According to the complaint, "Arthur Andersen viewed the loan accounting issue with regard to the apartment program as an opportunity to provide aggressive advice to the joint venture to encourage joint venture partner, BHSL, to replace its accountants, Touche Ross, with Arthur Andersen." In response to this, Andersen filed a motion for summary judgment, labeling the third-party action "an attempt by BHSL's directors to shift responsibility for their own management decisions to a professional firm whose advice they neither sought nor received."

Regardless of the legal maneuvering, which had the firms passing off blame on each other, the conversations and memos by and between Andersen and Touche partners led a senior government official to claim that "the Beverly Hills case provides a dramatic picture of how the Big Eight compete for business."

The power of the Big Six is not in making decisions for the corporations, governments and institutions they represent. Rarely do they decide issues unilaterally. Instead, their power comes from playing a critical advisory role in the decision-making process and ultimately providing a respected imprimatur that legitimizes management's actions no matter how outrageous they may be. In this way, their power extends beyond their clients and beyond the business community to the society at large, which looks at their signatures as an indication of financial integrity.

When a Big Six firm endorses a switch from equity to loan treatment, those who believe in the system of independent audits and who see the presence of the Big Six as an effective check and balance against management abuse take comfort in the veracity of the transaction. But as Congressman Dingell indicated in an exchange with Touche's Nelson Gibbs, this "comfort" can be open to question:

Dingell: What was it that caused Touche Ross to agree that these loans could be properly accounted for as loans rather than equity investments?

Gibbs: The change in the relationship between the two entities, the legal form of the transaction, and the cross-collateralization agreement.

Dingell: Were any of these properties making money?

Gibbs: Most of the properties were servicing all prior debt, and in that context there was positive cash flow.

Dingell: Positive cash flow. But were any of them making money?

Gibbs: Making money in a financial, accrual accounting sense, no.

Dingell: Okay. So in point of fact, money was moving through the books, but not enough to amortize the anticipated debt, is that right, to put it in layman's terms?

Gibbs: Yes, that would be a fair statement.

Dingell: So what they were doing, in point of fact, was really moving toward bankruptcy, is that right? When you have money moving through the books but not enough to pay off the debts, you are just moving slowly toward bankruptcy, or maybe you're moving very fast.

In its lawsuit against Touche Ross, the FSLIC has accused the firm of failing to disclose what it allegedly knew about BHSL's tenuous financial condition. The complaint reads, in part:

As a result of its engagement by BHSL, Touche had continual access to and knowledge of BHSL's confidential corporate and financial information. This included information that disclosed . . . the resulting failing financial condition of BHSL. Touche, in derogation of its responsibilities to BHSL, among other things, (a) failed to report BHSL's true financial condition and (b) approved accounting applications that were not in conformity with generally accepted accounting principles and that had the effect of artificially and inaccurately improving BHSL's financial condition as it appeared on its financial statements.

The complaint then goes on to make a most telling accusation, noting that without a properly performed audit, the regulatory checks and balances that are designed to safeguard the S&L system are rendered ineffective:

". . . had the regulatory agencies known the true facts, they would not have permitted BHSL to continue such business practices."

In many ways, the most extraordinary aspect of the fall of BHSL was that alarms had been sounding for years, but nothing of substance was done to reverse the thrift's slide. Even BHSL's internal auditor, Ellen Goodman, waved red flags about the thrift's practices. In a January 1983 interoffice memo, Goodman made the following observations:

We have completed nearly two years of audit procedures on the major loan files. The audit department findings,

McKenna's [McKenna, Conner & Cuneo, BHSL's outside legal counsel] findings and even the Leventhal [Kenneth Leventhal, a CPA firm specializing in real estate transactions] study all support the conclusion that remedial action is needed in major loan department operations. What is disturbing is not as much the severity of the errors as the volume of exceptions noted time after time. It would probably serve no useful purpose to correct most of the individual exceptions post mortem; however, the underlying fundamental issues do need to be addressed.

. . . I would categorize these recurring problems as
(1) Violation of association policy and procedures
(2) Violation of regulatory requirements
(3) Inconsistencies and questionable practices. . . .

Among the risks Goodman identified were "making a bad business decision based on incorrect or incomplete information." And she made these other shocking observations:

Staffing: It appears that everybody is conscientious and for the most part competent; however, the quality of the work is still lacking. With the rapid expansion of the department, it could just be that they are in over their heads with respect to organization, administrative abilities and technical expertise.

Regulatory Requirements: I have noted with one or two exceptions, no one in the major loan department has a copy of the California Guides. I recommend that several copies of these, and the regulations for other states in which the association conducts business, be maintained in the major loan department.

In summary, Goodman noted that the thrift had failed to act on similar recommendations made in the past. From her perspective, this was because of "the pressures of increased production and secondarily, because the department consists of deal makers and probably not administrators."

With Goodman having served as BHSL's internal auditor, and with a review of the internal controls a key part of the audit process, a critical question looms: Why weren't Goodman's concerns reflected in Touche's opinions? Touche Ross issued clean audit opinions in March 1983 for the year ended December 31, 1982, and in March 1984 for the year ended December 31, 1983. Touche lawyers say that the firm "did review the internal controls at Beverly Hills and utilized the results of that review in setting the audit scope. Ms. Goodman's concerns as expressed at the time were taken into account in the course of the review."

But did Touche go far enough?

The firm's national audit director stated the following about the auditor's role:

Independence of attitude and objectivity of judgment require that we assist the client to fairly and accurately represent the characteristics, risks and consequences of its legally authorized operations, or to adversely comment in our audit report on its failure to do so.

But with red flags waving, why didn't Touche report on the risks others saw so clearly?

For example, the problems at BHSL, and the threat they posed to the thrift's survival, were detected by a McKenna, Conner & Cuneo review of the major loan files in January 1983. After revealing a series of errors and deficiencies in BHSL's loan programs, a McKenna attorney made this ominous note:

One is led to wonder whether there are other mistakes or omissions which were not discovered by the association. Further, if there are so many errors and omissions, it is possible that a fatal one might occur at a future time.

Why didn't Touche Ross see this threat?

Touche's auditors appear to have accepted gaps in information concerning BHSL's activities that would be hard even for laymen to understand. In the process of restating BHSL's financials for 1983 (to show a downward earnings adjustment of $1.7 million), Touche reviewed the business files of former vice president Robert Newberry. Although no irregularities were found, a Touche auditor noted that the Newberry files presented to him by the thrift "were contained in eight cardboard boxes and were represented to me by G. Schrader, chief accounting officer, as being the complete set of files left by R. Newberry, except for one box which *was accidentally shredded*" [author's italics]. Although Touche would claim it was initially skeptical about the shredding, it was apparently assured by management that there was no reason for concern. But Congressman Wyden wasn't so certain:

> How can your firm be so sure in its conclusion that there were no irregularities when one of the eight boxes which contained relevant information was "accidentally shredded"? . . . Is the shredding machine at Beverly Hills big enough to shred an entire box of documents all at once, or do they have to feed the documents page by page?

Speaking for all those who have watched thrifts audited by the giant audit firms collapse soon after they were blessed, Congressman Wyden wondered aloud how an independent auditor could stand by and watch or, even worse, simply go along with the construction of an elaborate financial house of cards that ultimately consisted of nothing more than blue smoke and mirrors. When combined with an incredible series of poor investment decisions, mismanagement, and apparent self-dealing, the result was inevitable—total collapse.

Touche Ross's relationship with BHSL—which dated back to 1975, when Touche had replaced Peat Marwick as the thrift's auditors—finally unraveled in 1984. As Touche's national director of accounting and auditing standards stated at the public hearings:

> In July of 1984, we became aware of a possible compromising circumstance previously hidden from us. Over the new management's objections, we insisted on withdrawal of the association's [BHSL's] 1983 reports, public disclosure of the withdrawal, and appropriate notice to regulators. We then undertook additional audit procedures resulting in the restatement of the association's 1983 financial statements in November 1984, with a $1.7 million loss greater than was reflected in the earlier statements.
>
> Also, during this period of adjusting the 1983 statements, we noted and advised management that certain quarterly accounting practices in 1984 appeared to be inconsistent with GAAP and would likely have to be reversed—with negative effects on the association's operating results.

About a week after the financials were restated, Touche was dismissed as BHSL's auditor. According to Touche, this was the price it paid for the independence it had demonstrated by forcing BHSL to report the additional loss. But government sources noted "that Touche did not reverse itself on loan accounting in the restatement" and added that by the time Touche got religion, the situation was already out of hand.

According to former BHSL chairman Paul Amir, the search for a new auditor was launched because he had lost faith in Touche.

> I believe that new management has the right to change the auditors. When I was already in so-called control of Beverly Hills, and this was an uncontrollable company, so I wasn't in control really, I really compared the 10-K and the statement by Touche Ross to the actual, to the real world, what is happening in all this joint venture, real estate investments, and I thought that they were really far off the mark, so I was for changing them.

For whatever reason, Touche was terminated, and once the decision was made to fire the incumbent CPAs, management interviewed four contenders for the audit: Coopers & Lybrand, Arthur Andersen, Ernst & Whinney and Kenneth Leventhal. Because of its prominence in real estate, Leventhal was the early favorite, but it was dropped from consideration when Amir arrived at the conclusion that it was "not really a savings and loan auditor, so we shouldn't choose them."

In the end, E&W would get the nod, mostly because Amir thought "they were the most highly qualified," an opinion that may have been influenced by the fact that Amir was acquainted with one of E&W's Los Angeles–based partners. But in spite of E&W's good fortune, Coopers clung to the notion that it could still prevail. The firm's thinking on this reveals the extent to which the giant accounting firms are willing to scrounge for clients. Coopers partner Harold Schultz and Congressman Wyden had this exchange during the public hearings:

Wyden: Mr. Schultz, it is my understanding that you and a Mr. Frank Grau met with four auditors from the General Accounting Office on May 28, 1985. Who is Frank Grau?

Schultz: Frank Grau is the managing partner of the Coopers & Lybrand Los Angeles office.

Wyden: Did Coopers & Lybrand bid for the audit engagement after Touche Ross was dismissed or let go, however you would like to describe it?

Schultz: As I indicated in my testimony, we were involved in a proposal process in the fall of 1984.

Wyden: Was the audit engagement eventually given to Ernst & Whinney?

Schultz: Yes, it was.

Wyden: During your meeting with the General Accounting Office, Mr. Grau stated that he kept in touch with the management at Beverly Hills after the engagement there was given to Ernst & Whinney. That is correct, isn't it?

Schultz: I believe that is a statement he made, yes.

Wyden: Mr. Grau also stated that he kept in touch because he felt that Beverly Hills management might become dissatisfied with Ernst & Whinney since, in Mr. Grau's words, they had a tendency to raise their fees after coming in with a low bid. Is that correct?

Schultz: He made that statement, yes.

Wyden: Now, Mr. Grau made that statement. It is my understanding that the practice of coming in with a low bid to attract clients is known in the field as "lowballing." Is that correct?

Schultz: I presume that is one thing you could call it, yes.

As Coopers hoped, the relationship between BHSL and Ernst & Whinney soon unraveled, but the split had nothing to do with fees. Instead, E&W realized it had accepted a horrendous engagement fraught with serious risks, audit booby traps and an overall threat to its reputation.

In trying to make sense of BHSL's messy finances, E&W's auditors recognized the impropriety of treating the Stout ventures as loans. In arriving at this decision, E&W raised the following concerns:

> The borrower—Stout—had little or no equity in the projects and, therefore, in our view, was not "at risk." Because BHSL had advanced necessary funds, it was "at risk."
>
> BHSL did not have recourse to the borrower for repayment of the advances and could only look to the real property. In this regard, it should be noted that even though BHSL's advances to each real estate venture were secured by cross-collateralization provisions on all of the Stout projects, in most cases, BHSL's position was junior or subordinate to first or second mortgages.
>
> BHSL could only look to the ultimate sale of the property to recover its advances. It was not expected that the property would generate enough income to pay back the loans.
>
> The borrower was not required to make principal payments, but rather only interest payments.
>
> Although we did not complete the audit and thus did not obtain all of the documentation underlying the above transactions, we arrived at a preliminary view that the difference between applying the equity method, as we believed appropriate, and viewing the transaction as loans was somewhere between $20 million and $30 million.

As a result, Ernst & Whinney advised BHSL that it would have "to reverse certain amounts of accrued but uncollected interest income, recognize losses from the operations of certain real estate projects and defer any gain on sales of certain real estate." Clearly, this would have a negative impact on BHSL's financial statements.

What happened next is a matter of debate. According to E&W, its partner Alex Arcady tried to arrange meetings with the thrift's management. But in telephone conversations with BHSL, he encountered resentment at E&W's findings, up to and including the threat of a lawsuit.

From Arcady's perspective, both sides recognized they could not work together, E&W because it lacked the cooperation of senior management and BHSL because it could not accept the auditors' verdict on accounting standards. ". . . It was my impression," Arcady said, "that Beverly Hills had decided to shoot the messenger who had delivered the bad news."

But according to Paul Amir, Ernst & Whinney had recognized problems in the audit and simply wanted out:

> For a few weeks before the end of December [1984], I heard that our people have major problems with E&W. And then I received a call from a gentleman by the name of Erving Tow, whom I know was the main reason I voted for E&W, and he wanted to meet me. And we met on Christmas Day for early breakfast. And he says, "Paul, we would like to be relieved of this engagement. I think there are major problems in this association. There will be major losses in this association. We would like to get out of it."

Amir and Tow agreed to discuss the matter again in two weeks, but the second meeting proved equally fruitless. According to Amir, E&W expressed an even stronger desire to terminate the relationship, trying at this point to pass the engagement, like a hot potato, back to Touche Ross. As Amir recalled the meeting:

> I tried to convince them [E&W] to finish the audit or whatever it is. . . . He said, hey, you know the best thing for

Beverly Hills is if you go back to Touche Ross. I have no
choice. I say, "Okay, I will call up Touche Ross and if they
will accept us back, we will go back to Touche Ross."

We called, they had some conditions, and I, right there
at the audit committee meeting, put on the phone both
parties, Touche Ross and E&W, the managing partner of
E&W. And I thought we had some resolution.

The fact is, they didn't come to some kind of understanding. I don't believe Touche Ross was willing to take us back.
On the other hand, E&W claims that I dismissed them, so
we had to go out and look for another auditor.

At this point, Coopers & Lybrand, which had been waiting in the wings ever since Ernst & Whinney had first been
retained by BHSL, was asked to perform the audit. After
gaining assurances that the firm could conduct the audit
without interference by the client, and after consulting with
both Touche Ross and Ernst & Whinney, Coopers accepted
the engagement in February 1985.

Coopers quickly determined that many of the thrift's
assets were carried on the books at inflated values and
would have to be written down. The firm also stipulated
that BHSL would have to set aside additional loss allow-
ances. Based on this, Coopers stated in April 1985 that the
carrying value of the S&L's assets, "principally real estate
investments and loans collateralized by real estate, would
have to be written down by an amount which substantially
exceeded" the thrift's net worth. Bottom line: BHSL had
a negative net worth of approximately $65 million. (Ulti-
mately, BHSL's write-down would reach a total of approximately $400 million.)

Eight days later the FHLBB seized BHSL.

What was behind this shocking decline? Touche Ross
blamed both the thrift's management and the slumping real

estate market. "After a bitter takeover fight, a new management gained control of Beverly Hills in 1984," noted a Touche attorney. "According to figures provided by Coopers & Lybrand in its congressional testimony, Beverly Hills increased its deposits by more than $800 million between year-end 1983 and year-end 1984. In addition, new management increased Beverly Hills' holdings of junk bonds to approximately $300 million at year-end 1984. Moreover, the properties in the Stout Apartment Program were sold during 1984, which was much sooner than anticipated under the program and indicates that the program was abruptly terminated in a bad market. These factors, when combined with the declining real estate market in Southern California during 1984, caused a dramatic decline in Beverly Hills' financial conditions during 1984."

But according to a government official, two other factors were responsible for the decline of BHSL: "First, treatment of the Stout deals as loans enabled Beverly Hills to book a lot of income that wasn't there. All of this went straight to the bottom line, having the effect of artificially building up the thrift's net worth. Second, with the Stout deals treated as loans, Coopers had to look at the value of the assets used to collateralize them. And what they found was that these assets were highly inflated and had to be cut dramatically. When these two problems came home to roost, Beverly Hills proved to be a disaster."

Clearly, the carnage in the S&L industry cannot be blamed solely on the CPAs. As the auditors claim, thrift managements must be held primarily accountable for the practices that led to the failure of their institutions. There's no arguing that. But what is so troubling about the auditors' role in the S&L debacle is that they are licensed to maintain a higher standard, and ultimately to protect the public's interest. Here they have failed repeatedly. Forget the all-too-common excuse that complex fraud committed by devious management in collusion with others is hard to detect. To people who invest in thrifts or who entrust their life savings to them, this kind of don't-blame-us-if-the-bad-guys-are-real-smart buck-passing is hardly what they have in mind when they see a Big Six signature blessing a financial statement.

No one should know this better than the auditors. Unless they work harder to eliminate rather than excuse lapses in professional standards, the imprimaturs the public relies on, and that bring them billion of dollars in fees, will be worthless.

"The S and L crisis—which brought accounting integrity to the attention of Mr. and Mrs. Public—has led people to question the auditors' word," Congressman Wyden said. "More and more, they are wondering whether the watch-dogs are really watching out for anything but their own self-interest. Unless the system is strengthened, the audit profession will be headed for serious trouble."

Should that happen, Spicer & Oppenheim's former chairman Steve Oppenheim believes that part of the blame will have to be placed on the lack of accountability of certain Big Six partners. "The giants are so huge that the partners who work for them are anonymous," Oppenheim said. "They don't know each other, and they don't know each other's clients. When they get together to talk business, they have to wear nametags so they have some idea who they're talking to. From my perspective, that's no longer a professional firm. It's a big business.

"The problem is, in that big-business environment, no one is accountable. When the firm renders an opinion and that opinion turns out to be a mistake, the engagement partner claims he sent it to the review department. The review department, in turn, passes off responsibility to another department, and on and on. No one takes responsibility.

"From this standpoint, the Six-Pack reminds me of the Coca-Cola Company. Remember when Coke decided to replace its old standby with a new formula? Not a single executive in the Coke organization accepted responsibility for that disaster. In passing the buck down the line, they were indicating that the real culprit was the guy in the mailroom.

"The same thing happens with the big accounting firms. When things go wrong, none of the partners comes forward to take the blame. I guess we have to get the same message from them as we got from Coke: that when audits fail, the problem lies in the mailroom."

3

BAD BLOOD IN
THE HOUSE OF
ANDERSEN

When you have got an elephant by the hind leg, and he is trying
to run away, it's best to let him run.

—ABRAHAM LINCOLN

The stampede toward consulting that has transformed the
Big Six from accounting practices to a new breed of
consulting behemoths has brought turmoil in its wake. Although the firms cling to the designation "CPAs" because
of the access and the image of professionalism this imprimatur provides them, it is a misnomer. The fact is, the Big
Six are no longer "accounting firms." In a sense, they are
holding companies, a mix of semiautonomous service businesses functioning under a national brand name. This has
allowed growth through diversification—but at a price tag
that in Arthur Andersen's case (and in others to follow) may
prove exorbitant.

Today Arthur Andersen is a house divided, its accountants practicing under the name of Arthur Andersen, its
consultants doing business under the banner of Andersen
Consulting. Theoretically, these diverse professionals are

united by Andersen tradition, standards and culture. And while there is some truth to this, they have also been hostile camps, viewing each other with jealousy and suspicion. This is due, in great measure, to Andersen's success in creating a world-class consulting business—and in the process moving further away from its accounting roots than any of its peers have done. Thus the Catch-22 of Big-Six practice: Consulting, which is the wellspring of growth and profitability, can also be a harbinger of internal strife and dissension.

"To truly understand Andersen's troubles, you have to go back forty years, tracing the evolution of the big firms from 1948 to the present," said Victor Millar, until 1986 a senior partner responsible for Andersen's audit, tax and consulting practices. "Before 1948, the firms that would become the Big Eight were still small practices. The audit divisions, which got their first boost from the 1930s securities laws that required public corporations to be audited on an annual basis, were still new and modest in size. Consulting operations were lilliputian, generally less than a hundred people per firm, with most of the work focused on audit clients' financial systems."

It was not until the postwar period from 1948 to 1957 that the firms' audit practices began to experience substantial growth. Much of this growth came through multinational expansion as the Big Eight followed their clients in the global pursuit of business interests, in many cases moving into countries that had been our enemies in World War II. In addition, consulting began to extend its scope of services beyond financial-system engagements to a wider range of corporate assignments. This was particularly true at Andersen, where consultants made a critical breakthrough by tapping into the nascent technology of computerization, first by helping clients install and utilize the original IBM punch card equipment and then, in 1953, by applying their know-how to the early computer systems.

It was during this period that Millar joined Andersen directly out of the University of California at Berkeley, where he had earned an MBA degree. After two years in the audit division, he began to pursue his primary interest, computer consulting. The timing was right. As computers gained popularity with corporate management, they heralded a critical transition from manual to automated systems. This offered enormous opportunities for consulting practices, which would help clients facilitate the high-tech evolution to computerization. But at this point the Big Eight consultants—still the stepchildren of firms totally dominated by auditors—were hardly poised to take full advantage of the opportunities before them. Most of the practices were composed of a hodgepodge of specialists offering a smorgasbord of advisory services.

"At Arthur Andersen, we had eight separate consulting niches, including production control, cost accounting and operations research," Millar recalled. "The practice was poorly focused and, like its counterparts throughout the Big Eight, was a money loser—a drain on partners' earnings."

It was in this era that Andersen made a pivotal decision that years later would come back to haunt the firm. In the early 1960s, a rule requiring that newly hired Andersen consultants serve on the audit staff for a minimum of two years was rescinded. Until that critical change took effect, college graduates entering Andersen en route to consulting careers had first been indoctrinated into the rules and rituals of the audit culture. The message was clear: To be considered an Andersen professional, to be part of the fraternity, you had to think and act like an accountant. This, after all, was an accounting firm.

According to a high-ranking partner who was with the firm at the time, Andersen decided to change the rule primarily to appease the auditors who complained that they were training young people in the audit process, only to lose them to consulting as they moved along their intended career path. By eliminating the audit service requirement, Andersen thought it would be saving money and reducing turnover in the audit practice.

But in fact the firm was creating a monster. Over time, a growing faction of Andersen consultants would have nothing in common with their brethren in the audit practice.

"In the years when audit service was mandatory, those of us who joined the firm to be consultants struck up friendships with the auditors during the period we served with them," Millar recalled. "In most cases, these friendships continued throughout our careers, serving as a link between the audit and consulting practices. Because we had all been trained as auditors, we shared a common language and common values."

But this feeling of camaraderie began to fade as new classes of consultants moved into the Management Advisory Services (MAS) ranks without being exposed to the audit function. To this generation, the audit practice was unknown territory. Preoccupied with their own careers, they had little inclination to learn about life on the other side of the practice. Where before there had been two types of professionals functioning in a fraternal environment, now there were two separate factions, each following its own agenda.

From that time on, a gap developed at Andersen—a gap that would grow into a schism as audit and consulting changed places, the former enduring an agonizing decline in stature as the latter inherited the crown of the more glamorous and profitable practice.

The turnaround began as three negative factors affected the major accounting firms. First, the heady rise in audit revenues reached a plateau. Second, a rash of audit failures in the mid-seventies brought a flurry of massive lawsuits against the firms, heralding an era of costly litigation that would threaten the firms and drain their resources. And third, price cutting (commonly known as lowballing) cut deeply into profitability.

"At this time marketing was first emerging as an important factor," recalled Grant Gregory, former chairman of Touche Ross. "More than ever before, all of the firms were striving to grow, often at the expense of each other. In this competitive environment, one firm or another would get the idea that it could grow fastest by positioning itself as the discount auditor. It would tell clients, 'Choose us, we're the cheapest.' The idea was to play to the new price sensitivity in the audit market. That it did, but without the hoped-for benefit of giving any one of the firms an advantage. Because everyone played the game from time to time, all it did was slash the hell out of margins."

The firms entered the seventies assuming they were on a growth track that pointed in only one direction: up. At first their optimistic projection appeared to be on target. In the early part of the decade, growth remained strong. But what looked like business as usual was really an illusion. A heavy volume of major stock issues in the period masked the fact that the era of explosive growth had come to an end. Only when the oil crisis hit hard and the new-issues market nose-dived did the firms wake up to the fact that the gravy train had come to a halt. Suddenly, work dropped off and fees declined. What the dumbstruck auditors failed to realize—or failed to admit to themselves—was that they had changed from a growth industry to a mature industry.

Most responded by simply crossing their fingers and hoping the good old days would return.

While the princely auditors, spoiled by years of steadily rising profits, waited for a miracle, the consultants (always a scrappier lot, accustomed to searching for business) repositioned themselves to tap the full potential of the computer age.

"It was 1968 when a group of Andersen's high-ranking consulting partners came to the conclusion that our practice lacked focus, and that if it were allowed to remain that way, we would fail to capitalize on breaking developments in the marketplace," Millar said. "With this in mind, we held a series of meetings in Chicago, the purpose being to narrow down our practice scope from eight different areas to one or two high-priority, high-opportunity services. In effect, we were hashing out a strategic plan, saying, here's where we are now and here's where we want to be in five years, ten years and beyond."

The meeting proved to be a watershed for Andersen's consulting practice. Two critical decisions made at the time would, twenty years later, propel the firm's MAS division to the top of the Big Six.

First, Andersen's consulting executives recognized that their division was more of an affiliation of experts in various disciplines than a uniform, cohesive practice. As it was structured, each of the consulting practices had its own director at the Chicago headquarters and its own instructors at the firm's training facility in St. Charles, Illinois. Because the instructors were free to teach as they saw fit, the consulting disciplines reflected the unique styles and idiosyncracies of their respective faculty members.

To bring uniformity to the practice, Millar and a high-ranking team of consulting executives created a guidebook for teaching all of the consulting disciplines according to the "Arthur Andersen method." This done, the firm could pull together consultants from all over the world and assign them to an engagement, secure in the knowledge that they would approach the work according to a similar methodology. Because they had been trained under uniform guidelines, there was no need to bridge conflicting cultures or styles of practice. This ability to assemble cohesive teams around the globe gave Andersen a clear advantage.

Uniformity of practice was also a crucial factor in building the leverage pyramid that is so critical to professional firms, that is, the ratio of staff to partners. Because Andersen's MAS professionals had all been trained under the same guidelines, staff consultants could work without constant supervision from superiors. In practice, this meant that Andersen partners could have larger pools of people working under them, thus boosting the firm's leverage.

While most of Andersen's peers among the accounting firms were imitating the strategic-planning type of consulting practiced by McKinsey and Booz Allen Hamilton, Andersen was focusing on big computer systems engagements. This was critical to Andersen's higher leverage. Because strategic planning requires intensive partner involvement, it limits a firm's ability to leverage its practice. But Andersen's consulting business was just the opposite. Because it relied on teams of staff consultants with minimal partner involvement, leverage could soar.

"No one else among the big accounting firms understood the importance of intensive staff training," Millar added. "Competitors would look at our St. Charles facility and ask why we would invest so much money in a complex like that. They wondered aloud why we didn't simply hire experienced people from industry or from other firms. What they failed to see is that St. Charles was our key to leveraging and thus to building the most profitable practice in the Big Eight."

A second critical decision was to recognize that in the new era, all consulting disciplines were linked by the common thread of computerization. As the big manual systems were being replaced throughout corporate America, all of the Andersen consulting niches—production control, cost accounting, operations research—were becoming computer-based. Capitalizing on an emerging opportunity, Andersen made computer systems a foundation of its practice.

This full-scale assault on the computer-consulting market paid off handsomely in both prestige and profitability. As corporate CEOs committed millions of dollars to the giant IBM, RCA, GE and Honeywell mainframes that were automating their reservation systems, manufacturing processes and financial management, they sought outside experts to help install and implement their complex configurations of hardware and software. Because Arthur Andersen was the first firm to position its consulting practice as a giant SWAT team of computer experts and troubleshooters, it soon earned a reputation of being the "Marine Corps" of data processing.

"With that, Andersen started winning bigger and more complex engagements than any of the other firms could handle," said the MAS director for an Andersen competitor. "From the beginning, Andersen has been in a class by itself. Andersen's peers may be reluctant to admit it, but we all know it's true."

There was no denying that Andersen proved itself early on to be the smartest, most aggressive player in the new consulting game. Clearly, the firm recognized the huge potential of MAS practice and had positioned itself to benefit from it. But it was hardly alone. With the consulting practices growing two and three times as fast as auditing, and with clients willing to pay high-margin fees for this work, the managing partners of all but the most hidebound firms saw the future—and its name was Management Advisory Services.

But a major problem loomed ahead. Suddenly, the Securities and Exchange Commission (which has authority to oversee the accounting profession) was raising concerns over the widening scope of MAS practice. At issue was the question of "independence." Investors buying and selling shares of stock in publicly traded companies rely on "independent" auditors' opinions that companies' financial statements reflect their true financial condition. But as the SEC asked (echoing the sentiments of many observers), were the CPAs truly independent? Could an accounting firm selling a full menu of MAS engagements to a client be objective in auditing that client? Were there not clear conflicts of interest? Would the auditor bend to a client's will in order to protect its fees—not only audit fees (which were always a temptation) but also fees from the increasingly profitable MAS engagements?

Furthermore, could the CPA firms conduct objective audits when their clients' financial systems, or other facets of their operations, had been designed by the audit firms' consulting partners? To critics of the profession, including many in the nation's capital, the explosive growth of MAS practice threatened "independence"—and thus had to be curbed.

It was in this context that the SEC put the fear of God into the firms in 1979 by issuing the now-infamous accounting release 264. Designed to have a chilling effect on the wholesale expansion of MAS practice, the release urged the firms to limit that part of their practices not related to the audit function. To many inside the Big Eight, release 264 was but the first volley in a war that could lead, heaven forbid, to outright government regulation (as opposed to oversight) of the accounting profession.

Anxiety ran high, especially at Arthur Andersen, whose MAS fees already equaled 23 percent of the firm's total revenues, compared to 5 to 10 percent at its competitors. To further complicate matters, Andersen's aggressive and iconoclastic chairman, Harvey Kapnick, sought to move the firm in what was then considered to be a radical direction.

"Kapnick's idea was to split Andersen into two firms, auditing and consulting," recalled Gresham Brebach, then a partner in the Chicago office and chairman of the firm's technology advisory committee. "This would free the auditors to maintain a true-blue audit practice and, more important, would enable consulting to develop into a full-fledged service business that could venture into profitable niches as far afield from accounting as investment banking. Kapnick, a visionary leader who was clearly ahead of his time, foresaw the staggering growth in investment banking and wanted to play in that market."

But Kapnick's split-the-firm strategy, presented to Andersen's partners in September 1979, unleashed a furor. To the audit princes, who ran the firm with an iron fist, the idea of dividing up an accounting firm the way an industrial corporation spins off a subsidiary was anathema. The way they saw it, they would lose on several counts. Partners in charge (PICs) of Andersen practice offices feared the loss of consulting revenues, and the bulk of the auditors worried that the lack of consulting would put them at a disadvantage vis-à-vis their competitors, who could claim to serve a wider range of client needs.

Bottom line: Kapnick, who expected the firm to endorse his idea, found himself facing a palace revolt. "The audit partners feared that accounting release 264 was aimed directly at Andersen," said a former Andersen partner who was deeply embroiled in the controversy. "Because we were ahead of the pack in building a consulting practice, the auditors were convinced that the SEC intended to make an example of us, showing the big firms what would happen if they got too aggressive. As far as the CPAs were concerned, setting up a separate consulting division was just the thing that would get us into hot water with the SEC. They weren't about to let it happen."

Kapnick made the fatal mistake of looking so far into the future that he lost touch with the present. He failed to understand that a visionary is valuable to a professional practice only if he can convince his partners to share his vision and to work with him in pursuit of a common objective. But people skills were never Kapnick's strong suit. A tough-minded and brilliant man (the youngest, at age thirty, ever to be appointed an Andersen partner), he functioned more like a corporate CEO than like the head of a partnership. In doing so, he may have overlooked a critical difference: Unlike corporate underlings, his partners held the right to vote. When they rejected his plan to create separate practices, he resigned in October 1979—but not before planting the seed of an idea that would blossom forth with devastating impact a decade later.

The tempestuous conclusion of the Kapnick reign ushered in a new era at Arthur Andersen. After nearly a decade under Kapnick's electric leadership, the partners were ready for a steadier hand at the controls. As they searched the ranks for the ideal candidate, Duane Kullberg's name was on everyone's list. A dyed-in-the-wool auditor who had joined Andersen in 1954 and worked his way up from managing partner of the Minneapolis office to vice chairman of the firm, Kullberg enjoyed a reputation as a consensus builder. The polar opposite of Kapnick, he was quiet, stable, cautious—the ideal choice to heal the wounds and restore the collegiality that is the glue of a successful partnership.

"Kullberg was the antithesis of Kapnick," recalled Gresham Brebach, who would go on to become managing partner of U.S. consulting. "Where Kapnick was autocratic, Kullberg was democratic. Where Kapnick was decisive, Kullberg was indecisive. And where Kapnick made decisions single-handedly, Kullberg preferred management by committee."

As it turned out, Kullberg was the right man at the right time. Reflecting his faith in consensus-style management, he decentralized authority, giving more operating control to the functional heads of audit and MAS. Pleased that they would have greater control over their destiny, the consultants, who had bristled under centralized, audit-dominated management, were appeased—at least for the time being. And the auditors, who had rejected the idea of splitting Andersen in two, took solace in the fact that the new leader was inexorably opposed to any such drastic action.

With Kullberg installed as Andersen's CEO in February 1980, the firm got back to business, all hands attending to client service and practice development. On the surface, audit and MAS appeared to coexist peacefully. But deep in the ranks of the partnership, tensions were building. Still at issue were simmering conflicts over power and money. As the consulting practice continued to outstrip audit in terms of growth and profitability, the MAS partners resented their second-class status in the firm. Although they contributed far more to the bottom line than their peers on the audit side, they were held hostage to an archaic compensation system that assured virtual parity between the audit and consulting partners. Adding insult to injury, consultants held a minority presence on the Andersen board, and their top executive, Gresham Brebach, reported to an auditor, the area managing partner for North America.

The list of grievances went on and on. For example, only auditors could be partners in the firm. Although consultants were often referred to as "partners," technically they were "principals." Andersen's high command insisted that this was simply a matter of semantics, but according to the firm's partnership agreement, principals "shall have no right to vote on any matters presented to or requiring a decision or determination by the partners of the firm. . . ." In what could only be viewed as a weak-tea concession, the partnership agreement conceded that the principals "are permitted to cast ballots for the information of the partners."

Underlying the sticky issues dividing the two powerful Andersen factions was the growing conviction among a significant number of MAS professionals that they did not belong in the bowels of an accounting firm. Kapnick was right, they believed; MAS would be better served by breaking off from the mother lode. In part, this was an emotional response to an imbalance of power. But it was more than that. To the new generation of consultants—most of whom felt no kinship with the auditors—the rules, ethics and limitations imposed on them by the accounting practice were placing unnecessary restraints on their own business.

"By 1986, big-systems consulting was about a thirty-five-to-forty-billion-dollar-a-year business that was projected to soar to a hundred billion by 1992," Victor Millar said. "With no single firm controlling more than one percent of the business, it was clear that a period of consolidation was in the cards. But as far as I was concerned, it was equally clear that the big CPA firm consulting operations were not going to emerge from that consolidation as the industry leaders."

From Millar's perspective, the MAS practices of the big accounting firms were saddled with overwhelming problems, the most important being the "capital gap."

"A lot of people still think of consultants as a few bright guys with a pen and a pad," Milar said. "But when it comes to information consulting, that's not even close. This is a capital-intensive business, and unless you have access to substantial capital you cannot grow. Increasingly, contracts require that systems consultants buy the computer hardware up front and bill clients for it at the end of the engagement. It's a method clients use to shift the burden of financing onto the contractor. Considering that a single deal can require several million dollars and that we have many deals going simultaneously, you can see that there are very large sums of money involved."

Although public companies can raise capital by selling stock, this option is closed to accounting firms. For the most part, they must raise money from their partners. But what if those partners are not committed to expanding their firms' consulting practices? Then the practices fail to compete effectively with the big, independent consulting firms.

But the capital gap was only one of the serious problems dividing accountants and consultants in the big firms. Another came in the form of practice limitations. A growing trend in the systems consulting market called for consultants to engage in joint ventures with their clients. But an SEC rule banning CPA firms from engaging in joint ventures with audit clients put severe limitations on consultants. Rather than risk the loss of audit relationships, the big CPA firms blocked their consultants from engaging in these joint ventures, a limitation their competitors at independent consulting firms were not subject to. "We weren't CPAs, but as consultants in an accounting-firm environment, we were forced to live by the rules of CPAs," Millar said. "Rules that were having a negative impact on our business."

Because Andersen had the biggest, most profitable consulting practice—and the one, given its computer-systems orientation, most likely to forge business relationships with its clients—the ban against joint ventures aggravated the tensions between the auditors and the consultants. Goodwill and collegiality were giving way to the darker instincts of greed and jealousy. The way the consultants viewed it, the limitations imposed on their practice went beyond business and ethical issues. The auditors were holding them back, they suspected, not only because of SEC rules but also to protect their own egos. Fearful that they would soon be dominated by MAS, which was outstripping audit in growth and profitability, the auditors were thought to be building roadblocks to thwart the consultants' continued success. The perception that this small-minded jealousy was motivating the auditors threw oil onto the fire of an increasingly hostile relationship.

It was at this point, 1986, in the auditor/consultant tug-of-war that Millar, then Andersen's managing partner in charge of tax, audit and consulting, became the first high-ranking executive to defect from the firm. "At Andersen, I had a splendid job, running the biggest consulting practice in the world," he recalled, reflecting on his decision to abandon the Chicago giant. "Chances are I could have stayed there until mandatory retirement at age sixty-two. But as I looked around and took stock of what was happening at Andersen, I realized I had to leave.

"Why? In great part because I wanted to operate in an

environment where people didn't feel threatened by my success. Where the consulting practice could get bigger and bigger without anyone resenting us for it. The more I thought about it, the more I wanted to work in a place where the main activity was consulting and where everyone was committed to it. That wasn't Andersen. I was in the right business, just the wrong orchard."

In December 1986, Millar left Andersen, accepting a $1-million-a-year post as CEO of Saatchi & Saatchi Consulting, an upstart venture launched by the Saatchi brothers, a London-based sibling act that through a series of bold acquisitions had quickly assembled the largest network of advertising agencies in the world. With their focus shifted to the lucrative consulting market, the Iraqi-born brothers gave Millar a mandate: to make lightning strike again by creating the world's largest consulting operation.

Although the Saatchis had offered to buy Andersen's MAS practice in 1985, at that point Andersen's senior officers had failed to see Saatchi as a threat to their interests. Nor were they particularly troubled by Millar's defection. As a gesture of goodwill for a departing executive, Kullberg hosted a farewell dinner party for Millar, inviting Andersen managers and board members to his home for an evening of fond farewells. "It was a warm and friendly gesture, and I felt wonderful about it," Millar remembered. "Everyone reminisced about the years we'd spent together and wished me good luck in my new position. Duane and the other senior executives couldn't have been more gracious."

But an era had ended. This was the last time an Andersen consultant of Millar's stature would depart under friendly terms. The next would be savaged in the press and bombarded with lawsuits.

* * *

Shortly before Millar's departure, Kullberg—alert to the ever-louder rumblings in the ranks—had appointed a "Mix of Services Committee" to advise management on the proper balance among audit, tax and MAS services. "The committee's job was to address the mission of the firm," Brebach said. "To no one's surprise, it concluded that audit should be the core of the practice. All major decisions concerning staffing, investments and deployment of personnel should be made with the objective of remaining a premier audit firm. This was a direct attack on consulting. If the auditors were to continue making all the key decisions about the use of Andersen's resources, they could slow the growth of consulting, thus keeping our practice subservient to theirs."

The committee came up with a matrix of options for resolving the increasingly bitter feud that was pitting partner against partner, practice against practice. The firm could: (1) spin off the MAS practice, (2) spin off the large-scale systems practice, leaving the rest of the MAS practice as it was, or (3) spin off the audit practice.

According to Brebach, "The committee presented the three options, but the members never seriously considered spinning off the audit practice. From the beginning, they were in favor of spinning off the large-scale systems practice. They'd found the devil, and the devil was precisely that part of the firm's consulting practice that accounted for the great bulk of the fees and that virtually supported the firm, making up for the losses the audit division was generating. The committee, which was dominated by auditors, was biased from the start. It echoed the auditors' party line that spinning off the large-scale systems practice would solve all of Andersen's problems. By jettisoning this segment of the practice, we would get the SEC off our backs and would put an end to the jealousies and the strains that were splitting the firm."

The first of three meetings convened to discuss the strategies recommended by the Mix of Services Committee was held in Williamsburg, Virginia. Known internally as "Williamsburg One," the session proved to be a disaster for the MAS partners. A statement developed at the conference declared that auditing would remain the core of the firm. Irate at what he considered insensitive and high-handed treatment, Brebach (joined by other senior consultants) demanded that the report be rewritten. His demand was rejected.

"It was after this meeting that the consultants recognized the need to draft our own mission statement," Brebach said. "We had been telling the firm's management that to maintain our position as major players in the big-systems arena, we had to invest money, engage in joint ventures and pay competitive salaries. To which they responded, time and again, that we really didn't need any of that. Based on their myopic view of the world, we were doing fine, we had great profits, so why rock the boat? Their attitude was that we should crawl back into our holes and leave them alone. We could ask for change, for resources, for clout in the firm, but we weren't going to get any of it."

Determined to challenge this, a group of MAS leaders set out to write a mission statement of their own. As part of this process, they explored eight possible strategies for the future of Andersen's consulting practice:

1 Business as usual: The consulting line organization would continue to report to the local-office PICs (mostly auditors).
2 Regional structure: Each geographic region would have

tax, accounting and consulting chiefs, all reporting to a regional director (an auditor).

3 National business unit: The consulting line organization would report to five regional consulting partners, who in turn would report to a national consulting partner. This person would report to a national managing partner (an auditor).

4 Strategic business unit: Similar to the national business unit except that the national consulting partner would report directly to the chairman, with no intervening auditors in the chain of command.

5 Separate financial unit: Similar to the strategic business unit, with the major exception that consulting would be a separate legal entity with its own financial structure. Instead of pooling income with the other practices, consulting would pay a percentage of its fees back to audit.

6 Third-party minority: Sell a minority interest in the consulting practice to a third party. Its income would no longer be pooled with tax and audit.

7 Third-party majority: Same as the above, except that the sale would be of a majority interest.

8 Sale of the entire consulting division.

Brebach and his supporters felt the best choice was the separate financial unit, and in July 1987, Brebach presented this goal to a London meeting of Andersen's senior consulting partners from around the world. "We viewed this meeting as a forum for putting all of our ideas on the table," Brebach recalled. "As far as we were concerned, it was an open session. Anything and everything could be discussed. We even broached the idea of a name change—of calling the MAS group Andersen Consulting. It was our way of exploring the issues openly and candidly. But where the consulting executives saw an exchange of ideas and an attempt to resolve a serious schism in the firm, the auditors could see only treason. At a break in the meeting, a senior auditor placed an urgent call to Kullberg, telling him, 'We have a revolt on our hands. We must act now to quash it! There's no time to waste!' "

Soon after, Kullberg summoned five executives, identified as the consultants' "ringleaders," to an emergency meeting in Chicago, where they were called before the firm's operations committee and board of directors. According to Kullberg, the purpose was simply to air some of the issues raised at the London meeting. But Brebach saw it differently.

"We felt as if we were facing an inquisition," he said. "Weinbach [Andersen's chief operating officer] was especially tough, firing a battery of questions at us. Clearly, he didn't think we had the right to be discussing options for the consulting practice. Between the lines, he was accusing us of insubordination. We said, that's crazy. There'd been no secrets. Everyone knew the meeting was taking place. But no matter what we said, they weren't listening. They preferred to see something sinister, and they saw it. That's the way Andersen auditors related to Andersen consultants."

A time bomb was ticking, and in short order it would blow up in everyone's face.

The critical issue in the conflict between Arthur Andersen's consulting and accounting practices centered around the consultants' demand for autonomy and how that autonomy would be achieved. Under the Andersen setup (and this was standard throughout most of the big accounting firms), the firm was governed day to day by the partner in charge of the local offices. The PICs, most of whom were auditors, controlled all aspects of the practice including the audit and MAS budgets, salaries, raises, promotions and client service—a classic case of the establishment protecting its position by dominating the key functions. Yes, the firm could venture into lucrative sidelines, but the auditors insisted on retaining the power they had always held and keeping the consultants under their control.

"As consulting engagements grew in size, we often had to pull together people from four or five offices to serve a client," Millar recalled of the days well before Brebach's "insubordination." "No problem, except that if a PIC questioned the merits of the engagement, he could throw a wrench into the works. If he didn't want his people traveling out of town, or if he wanted them to be available for a local client, he would do his best to torpedo the consulting engagement even if it brought much more money to the firm than the local audit.

"The system was riddled with sideways reporting to people who seemed intent on gumming up the works. In the position I had before leaving the firm, the entire Arthur Andersen organization reported to me on a dotted-line basis. But—and this is an important 'but'—the organization chart had the consultants, accountants and tax people reporting to the PICs on a straight-line basis."

As a practical matter, if Millar wanted to staff a particular client engagement by relocating personnel, he had to get approval from the PICs before he could say yes to the client. Under this setup, the auditors had enormous influence over the course and direction of the consulting practice. As consulting became bigger and bigger, Millar found this situation to be more and more intolerable.

Were MAS to be reorganized as a national business unit (one of the eight options listed on the mission statement of the Brebach group), consultants would be able to reroute their reporting relationship from the local-office PICs to the regional MAS partners, who in turn would report to a national MAS partner. Only at this high level would MAS report to the national managing partner in each country. The idea behind this proposed restructuring was to remove the auditors' pervasive influence over the consultants. An improvement for the consultants, yes, but the Brebach faction favored even greater autonomy; they wanted to organize the consulting practice as a separate financial unit.

It was here that they ran into opposition from chief operating officer Larry Weinbach, who had approved the national business unit but objected to the separate financial unit. "In the battle between the auditors and the consultants, Weinbach served as the point man for the accountants' side," said David Lord, editor of *Consultants' News*. "It was set up this way so that the CPAs could have a strong leader voicing their interests. But with Weinbach representing one flank and Brebach another, they were bound to clash."

In the end, Kullberg approved the national business unit as a compromise move that gave the consultants considerable autonomy without the purse-string independence of a separate financial unit. Effective September 1987, Gresham Brebach—until that point the head of the New York consulting practice—was installed in the post of managing partner of U.S. consulting.

Although the compromise fell short of the consultants' ultimate goal of a truly independent practice unit with autonomous finances, progress had been made. "For the first time we had real power in resource deployment," Brebach said. "We didn't have to worry about getting auditor approval to move consultants from point A to point B. On a more fundamental level, the cultural bias that required auditors to oversee consultants had been broken.

But with that move an accounting firm tradition, one that had always given the CPAs the trump card in firm politics, was also threatened."

It was a threat the auditors took seriously, complaining to Kullberg that he had gone too far to appease the MAS partners. Faced with a mounting backlash from the auditors and the tax partners, Andersen management had second thoughts about the compromise ironed out with the consultants. Executives at the highest levels began to worry that they had been coerced into taking an action they had never really intended to take—and breaking a tradition they had never intended to break.

"They started to fear that this might be the first step in a chain reaction that could lead to the loss of the consulting practice," said a former high-ranking Andersen partner. "And they worried that if that happened, they would have nothing to sell to clients save for tax services and a stagnant audit practice. This put the fear of God in them."

It was a fear that could also be traced to a spring 1987 breakfast meeting between Duane Kullberg and Victor Millar, now head of Saatchi & Saatchi Consulting. Empowered with a Saatchi mandate to expand the business through major acquisitions, Millar had set his sights on his former employer.

"Before I left Andersen, Duane and I had talked about the strains in the consulting practice," Millar said. "I brought this up again at our breakfast meeting, saying I was now in a position to acquire companies and it might be a good way to address those strains. I made the case that I was the best person to buy Andersen's consulting unit because I understood the value of St. Charles and because I knew what it would take to look after the interests of the consulting partners.

"It was a cordial meeting. Duane said he was exploring other approaches, but he agreed that we could meet again at a later date. In the meantime, I asked if he would send me the firm's earnings figures, so that I could frame a dollar offer the next time we got together."

But the financial data never came, and after repeated calls to set up another meeting went unanswered, Millar sent a telegram to Kullberg and the Andersen board, restating his interest in buying the consulting practice. Soon after, the board responded with a telegram of its own, stating that it was not interested in a sale and, furthermore, that any attempt by Saatchi to press the matter would not be taken kindly.

"Because we had no intention of mounting a hostile offer, which in a partnership would mean trying to incite a mass defection of the partners," Millar said, "we ceased our efforts regarding an acquisition of Andersen's consulting practice. For me it became a dead issue."

But another event would add to Andersen's trepidation over its consulting practice. At the same time the consulting/accounting schism was splitting the firm down the middle, an outsider with an entrepreneurial interest in building a major consulting practice convened a secret meeting of a number of the big firms' MAS partners at New York's La Guardia Airport. It was here that Stephen Page, a London-born technology consultant–turned–executive recruiter, tried to convince the partners to defect from their firms and join him in starting a new practice.

The idea had been born in 1982, when Page's Dallas-based search firm, Page-Wheatcroft & Co., had been engaged to help Arthur Young recruit as many as twenty senior consulting partners for its information technology practice. Through this work, which continued for several years, Page made contact with hundreds of consultants in the big accounting firms, learning from them how their information technology practices were organized, how they served clients, how the partners were compensated. In the process, he discovered that there was a great deal of dissatisfaction in the firms, mostly over the compensation issue. The biggest bone of contention was that salary structures failed to reward superior performance.

"For example," Page said, "the star salesmen—guys who were bringing in twenty to fifty million dollars' worth of business—were getting paid only forty thousand dollars a year more than the guys who were bringing in two to three million. Because the big CPA firms weren't willing to establish the kind of incentive-based compensation systems they needed to attract the top consultants, I knew they would face difficult times down the road. So I made a proposition to the partners in charge of Arthur Young's information technology practice: Why not be the first firm to establish a separate consulting practice under the control of the consulting partners? The way I saw it, the accountants could retain equity in the firm, but the consultants would own more than fifty percent of the practice. My initial contacts at AY liked the idea, but when they took it to chairman Bill Gladstone, he apparently pooh-poohed it."

It was at this point, in the spring of 1987, that Page decided to expand his horizons and put together a new firm composed of information technology stars from all of the big CPA firms. With this in mind, he sent what was intended to be a top secret letter to the one hundred leading Big Eight consultants, asking them to explore the idea of forming a new firm. These superstar performers, he thought, would have much to gain by joining an organization free of auditor control, free of auditor/consultant conflicts in pitching new business and free of the anemic compensation packages that kept consultants in relative parity with the auditors even though they were making the lion's share of the profits.

"Page had a wonderful fantasy of creating a dream firm composed of the best people from all of the big accounting-firm consulting practices," said David Lord of *Consultants' News*. "Because he saw that the future of the consulting business would be in publicly financed, highly growth-oriented firms, he recognized that splitting off from the accounting giants and creating an independent entity had great potential."

But Page's plan was derailed for two reasons. First, in addressing the envelopes for his "secret" letter, a secretary mistakenly typed the name of an Arthur Andersen audit partner rather than the consulting partner of the same last name to whom it was supposed to go.

"As soon as Andersen's top management learned of my letter," Page recalled, "they turned up the heat, making it clear to their partners that they knew what I was doing and that it would be unwise for anyone to participate with me. They were really worried about this, as were their counterparts at the other giant CPA firms. In fact, one of Andersen's top people said about me, 'Never before has one man managed to upset so many people at one time.' "

Even with his cover blown, Page managed to hold that meeting in the summer of 1987 with a small group of consultants at the Admirals Club at New York's La Guardia Airport. It was here that the executive recruiter faced his most difficult hurdle. "The guys at the meeting were enthusiastic about my idea and were willing to join in with me, but only if their salaries would be guaranteed," Page recalled. "I'd gone into this plan thinking that I'd be dealing with entrepreneurial-type people, but I wasn't even close. These men were earning $250,000 to $350,000 a year. They were in their late thirties to early forties, had just bought

$500,000 homes and had two or three kids in college. They weren't about to take a financial risk at this point in their lives."

Although Page made repeated attempts to find a financial backer for his plan, the deals fell through—including one that would have provided enough money to get the new firm off the ground. "I made contact with a prominent British financier who considered putting up fifty million dollars for the deal," Page said. "We had several meetings in Europe, and each time it looked as if we would agree on terms. But then, inexplicably, he dropped out. While this was going on, the chairmen of the Big Eight were hearing about it and I was threatened, through various channels, with litigation. I even heard that Andersen had prepared a lawsuit claiming interference in their business, and that the suit would be filed if I didn't cease my activities. Let me tell you, I wish they had sued. It would have brought my plan to center stage, putting it squarely in the public eye."

With attackers circling its most profitable practice, Andersen's management now turned to the prominent law firm of Fried, Frank, Harris, Shriver & Jacobson to structure what was termed an "antitakeover clause" to be added to the partnership agreement. "This was the now-infamous noncompete clause," Brebach said. "Management claimed that the clause was designed to protect the practice from a takeover, but that was nonsense. With a partnership, you can't simply tender for shares and—puff—the firm is yours. You can take over a partnership only if the partners want to be taken over. And that wasn't the case at Andersen. We all knew about the meeting between Millar and Kullberg. They may have thought it was a secret, but it wasn't.

Still, we didn't respond by rushing up to management hollering, 'Sell the practice! Sell the practice!' Nothing like that went on."

According to Weinbach, the noncompete clause was simply a way of protecting the firm's legitimate interests. "We knew that people were making offers for our consulting practice," he said, "and we didn't want those offers to create havoc in the firm. We knew we couldn't stop people from leaving the firm, but if they did, we wanted to make sure they didn't take clients or proprietary information with them. I thought we had every right to seek this protection."

But from the consultants' perspective, the noncompete clause violated the spirit of partnership. "The prospect of a noncompete clause made the Andersen consulting partners feel as if they were being treated like children," says David Lord of *Consultants' News*. "They resented the fact that they would be bound by law to the firm."

Incensed by the noncompete rules, which were recommended by Andersen's Board of Partners in October 1987, Brebach wondered just how enforceable they would be if they were voted on by the full partnership. Asking around informally, he got conflicting advice. Some said the courts would throw out the rules on the grounds that they restricted an individual's ability to seek gainful employment. Others countered that because Andersen had every right to protect its client base, the rules would stand up in litigation. Brebach was more confused than ever.

In March 1988, Brebach took off for a ski vacation in Colorado. There he ran into a former Andersen tax partner, who suggested that the prominent Chicago law firm of Kirkland & Ellis be allowed to to review the noncompete clause. Taking his advice, Brebach (acting on his own, rather than as a representative of Arthur Andersen) met with a Kirkland & Ellis partner, asking him whether or not the clause was legally enforceable and, if so, what could be done to modify it. As Brebach feared, the lawyers left little to cheer about. According to Kirkland, the clause was skillfully crafted and appeared to be airtight. From all indications, it would stand up in court.

It was in this context that Brebach and a cabal of Andersen's senior consulting partners held a secret powwow at New York's "21" Club in April 1988. The session had all the earmarks of a corporate mutiny. The meeting was called to marshal the forces of opposition against the proposed noncompete clause, and also to make it clear how much money the consulting division could fetch if it were to be sold on the open market.

"We knew that Andersen's chief operating officer, Larry Weinbach, had asked Goldman Sachs to assess the value of the consulting practice," Brebach said. "But when I asked Weinbach and CEO Duane Kullberg what the numbers were, they refused to say. Appeals to Goldman also turned up dry. Thinking that the consulting partners had a right to know the value of the practice they were running, I asked a friend at Morgan Stanley—which happened to be one of our clients at the time—if he would put a price tag on a hypothetical computer-systems consulting practice with a hundred and fifty partners, three thousand professionals and three hundred million dollars in revenues. This hypothetical practice was smaller than Andersen's but would give the investment bankers a model for coming up with a pretax earnings multiple that could be extrapolated to Andersen's consulting practice, thus giving us an approximate value.

"We weren't suggesting that the practice be sold. We were just exploring all the options: whether we should accept the noncompete clause or, if we rejected it, what alternatives were at our disposal. Clearly, a sale of the consulting practice was a possibility we could recommend to Andersen management, but we never discussed that at the meeting."

Cloistered inside the "21" Club, the Brebach-led Andersen contingent discussed and debated the hated non-compete clause, ultimately arriving at the conclusion that they could not coexist with it. If it were to be made part of the firm's bylaws, they decided, they would resign. Convinced that they were indispensable to Andersen's consulting practice and that neither CEO Kullberg nor the Andersen board would jeopardize the stability of the firm's biggest and fastest-growing division—$1.1 billion in revenues at the time—they thought their decision carried little risk. Faced with a unified show of force, management would have to back down, withdrawing the proposed clause.

To be truly effective, Brebach's showdown strategy called for a surprise attack. With this in mind, one of the consulting executives placed a call to Kullberg's Chicago office to arrange an urgent meeting between the chairman and his senior MAS executives. Once face to face with Kullberg—who ran Andersen from behind the closed doors of his modest office—they would spring the ultimatum: Withdraw the onerous amendment or face the risk of our resignations. It was a power play the rebels were confident would succeed.

Thus the showdown with Kullberg was set. In a matter of weeks, the CEO would learn for the first time of the budding insurrection in the executive ranks. Or so Brebach and his contingent thought. The fact was that the Andersen firm, always a secretive operation driven by a Nixonian paranoia that saw enemies behind every door, was run more like a bugged embassy than a gentlemanly professional practice. If the brain trust of the consulting practice were to plot behind the CEO's back, chances are he would know about it.

He did. Without the knowledge of those in attendance at the "secret" meeting at the "21" Club, an informant in the ranks—to this day, Brebach says, the mole's identity remains a mystery—placed secret telephone calls to Kullberg, posting the chairman on the group's deliberations and alerting him to the plan for a surprise ultimatum. Thus, when the insurgents met with Kullberg, he would be ready for them with a strategy of his own. But for the time being, he camouflaged his knowledge of the "secret" events leading up to the meeting.

The meeting was held in a conference room next to Kullberg's office. The furnishings were Spartan, reflecting the CEO's personal style. He was not a man who surrounded himself with the trappings of power. There were no antiques or artworks. This was very much an accountant's conference room.

Brebach and his cohorts faced a somber greeting, none of the usual small talk. In fact, hardly a word was said. Duane Kullberg sat at one end of the rectangular conference table, Larry Weinbach at the other. The five consulting partners who had come to make their presentation sat between them.

"Getting right down to business, we told Kullberg that the noncompete clause had to be withdrawn," Brebach recalled. "That we simply couldn't live with it. We told him it was unfair, it was unnecessary and it was a sham. To our way of thinking, it was management's way of taking away our leverage. The consulting partners wanted greater power in the firm and in turn a greater voice in our own destiny. We'd started our own planning process, and we knew firm management saw this as a threat. The noncompete clause was just a device to limit what power we had in lobbying for change within Andersen. Without the option of leaving the firm and competing for the clients we'd been serving, we had no leverage.

"In two recent episodes, consulting partners had left the firm, taking clients and personnel with them. Andersen had tried to halt this but had lost both cases in arbitration. The noncompete clause had been designed to put an end to this, yes, but that was only the official reason. Beneath the surface, the auditors feared that we were becoming too independent and were no longer subservient to them. So they used the noncompete clause as a club over our heads. We expressed all of this at the meeting."

As far as the Brebach contingent could tell, Kullberg appeared to be giving his senior consulting managers a fair hearing. He listened quietly throughout the session, jotting down an occasional note as those assembled ticked off their litany of complaints.

"Kullberg agreed to establish a forum for settling a number of the key issues we presented to him," Brebach said. "That alone was a major breakthrough. Until that time, when consulting partners wanted to air their opinions or get something done for their practice, they'd had to navigate through a cumbersome bureaucratic process complete with roadblocks set up by the auditors. But because the new forum would allow us to meet directly with Kullberg and Weinbach, we thought it would be very helpful in solving the issues that divided the consulting practice from the rest of the firm.

"So we left the meeting feeling we had made some progress. Kullberg agreed to consider our request to withdraw the noncompete amendment, and he promised we would be hearing from him shortly. Judging by the compromising spirit he displayed at the meeting, we expected the amendment to be withdrawn. But at that point, all we could do was wait."

Aware that Kullberg was attending a May board meeting at Andersen's international headquarters in Geneva, Brebach assumed the CEO would use the opportunity to withdraw the now-infamous amendment. It was with a sense of heightened anticipation that Brebach waited for a phone call from Geneva. "I expected a friend of mine on the board to call with the good news, but the phone never rang. Throughout the course of the meeting, I heard from no one. Naturally, my spirits sank. But just as I was about to give up hope, I got the call I'd been waiting for. On May 16, my contact on the board called to say that the amendment had been withdrawn. That call was music to my ears."

But the music didn't last long. Just days later, Weinbach stopped by Brebach's office to suggest that he meet with Kullberg the following morning. When Brebach mentioned that he was scheduled to attend a client meeting, Weinbach strongly suggested he cancel it. "He said, 'It's important that you be here!'" Brebach recalled. "From the tone of his voice, I guess I should have known something grave was afoot, but I didn't. Looking back now, it's clear I misread all the signs. I thought the purpose of the meeting was to notify me officially that the amendment had been withdrawn and to put all the issues on the table so that we could address them one by one."

But instead Brebach walked blindfolded into an ambush. As soon as he entered Kullberg's office, he could tell something was wrong. Kullberg was seated behind his desk, Weinbach on a side chair. Both were stone-faced. The mood was that of a military court-martial.

"Still, Kullberg's first comments were positive," Brebach recalled. "He broke the silence by saying, 'We want to let you know that the amendment has been put aside for now.'

That was just what I wanted to hear. Perhaps I'd jumped to conclusions. Perhaps nothing was wrong. Maybe all the news was good news after all. Perhaps Kullberg and the board recognized that the consulting partners had to be appeased. That we had to have a greater voice in the firm."

For a brief, heady moment Brebach indulged in the thrill of victory. The ultimatum had succeeded. Whatever his personal feelings about the noncompete clause, Andersen's CEO apparently feared the loss of his top consulting partner. He had caved in.

Or had he? Looking away from Brebach as he spoke, Kullberg sprang a surprise attack of his own. "We've decided to relieve you of your duties, Gresh," he said in words Brebach would never forget. "Effective today, you are no longer in charge of the firm's consulting practice."

Brebach had been poleaxed. Coming from Kullberg, this sudden, calculated dismissal was shocking.

"I'd always considered Duane to be a fair and reasonable man," Brebach said. "So for him to cut me down like that, without due process, was terribly upsetting. All I could think was that Weinbach was behind it. I'd known for some time that he saw me as a threat, and I could only assume that my abrupt dismissal was a reflection of that. With consulting having become the moneymaking core of the firm, it was likely the top consulting partner would be competing with Larry for the CEO's position once Duane's term was over. I think Larry saw my dismissal as a propitious way of eliminating his most serious competitor."

Weinbach later denied Brebach's allegation, noting that he had appointed Brebach to the position of head of U.S. consulting. "Would I have done that if I viewed the man as a threat?" Weinbach asked.

According to Kullberg, the firing was entirely his own decision, one he had reached after obtaining a copy of the

"21" Club agenda. Judging by the items on the agenda and by conversations with a number of the participants at the meeting, Kullberg concluded that Brebach and the others aligned with him were trying to segregate, or buy out, the cream of the consulting practice. To his way of thinking, that kind of action on the part of a few simply violated the spirit of the Andersen partnership and had to be dealt with firmly.

Facing Kullberg's icy death sentence, the normally un-flappable Brebach found himself off balance, groping for answers. He remembered the confrontation this way:

> Brebach: Relieved of my duties? Just like that? Don't you think this deserves further explanation?
>
> Kullberg: We know all about your meeting at the "21" Club. It's inappropriate for a partner of this firm to be hiring outside counsel without the approval of management. It defies the spirit of partnership. What's more, we have evidence that you were proposing to take over part of the consulting practice.
>
> Brebach: That's preposterous! Who told you that? Did you check with all the people at the meeting? Did all of them tell you that?
>
> Kullberg: We have a copy of the agenda, and we have spoken with a number of people in attendance.
>
> Brebach: And you are determined to dismiss me on that basis? On the reports of anonymous sources?
>
> Kullberg: I repeat: Effective today, you are relieved of your duties.

Watching a twenty-four-year career vanish before his eyes, the bitter, frustrated, shell-shocked consulting executive fought back the only way he could: "The actions you are taking today," he said, "won't solve the problems of this firm. It will only exacerbate them. Mark my words, this will come back to haunt you."

Kullberg would remember that there was less give-and-take in their confrontation, that Brebach was visibly angry but left the room in a matter of minutes. Whatever was said, and whoever said it, Brebach was out.

Acting on the "bad apple theory," Kullberg had removed the "cancer" from the ranks, certain that this would nip the "insurrection" in the bud and quickly restore tranquility to the firm. But he underestimated the consultants' rage over their status in the firm, over the noncompete clause and over their inability to secure a higher level of autonomy. Brebach's dismissal, taken as a sign of consulting's impotence in the face of the auditors' raw power, unleashed a furor.

"The consultants took Brebach's departure as further evidence that they had to have a separate practice," David Lord said. "Not, as Brebach will tell you, because they adored him and considered him indispensable. In a consulting firm like Andersen's, there are two many giant egos for one man to loom so large. But on the other hand, Brebach was an outspoken leader for the consultants' interests. Although many of his colleagues considered him to be too brash and rebellious, they agreed with his position and saw his dismissal as a collective slap in the face."

With Andersen more divided than ever, Kullberg was under siege, buffeted on one side by the consultants, who were pressing their case for two separate firms, on the other by the audit and tax partners, who were arguing that he had done the right thing and should hold his ground. In this adversarial environment, Kullberg was hardly the kind of Lincolnesque figure who could bring the two sides together and patch up the differences between them. Instead, he sanctioned a "Change Management Task Force," giving it a mandate to come up with proposals for reorganizing the firm. In a plan delivered to the partnership in the winter of 1988 (and approved by the partnership in January 1989), management attempted to appease the consultants by agreeing to create a separate entity, Andersen Consulting, that would be backed by a $10 million advertising campaign and an agreement that the consultants would have a separate profit pool (limited, however, by the fact that they would have to contribute to tax and audit should those divisions' profits drop below a certain point). All in all, the consultants had won a major victory, getting the separate financial unit they had sought at the outset.

Andersen's move represented a major breakthrough for accounting-firm consultants. For the first time, an MAS practice had moved out from under the oppressive thumb of the auditors and begun to operate under its own brand name, organizational structure and compensation system. Under the terms of the reorganization:

- Andersen was divided into two divisions, audit/tax and consulting.
- The board of partners of Swiss-based Société Coopérative, the ruling body of Andersen's worldwide organization, was expanded from eighteen to twenty-four members, with consulting's presence increasing from six to seven seats.
- The traditional chain of command, whereby consultants reported to auditors from the local-office level and up, was reoriented. Now consultants would report to their peers all the way up to the managing partner of worldwide consulting, which became a separate financial unit. Andersen Consulting was granted full status as a member

firm of Société Coopérative, on an equal footing with Arthur Andersen (accounting) and all other international member firms.

Although the auditors still retained the ultimate veto (as it was structured, the Andersen Consulting managing partner reported to Andersen's CEO, traditionally an auditor), the creation of Andersen Consulting and the liberalization of the salary rules satisfied the consultants for the time being.

But Duane Kullberg, who had become a symbol of the conflict between the practices, still found himself under siege. Eyed with suspicion by both the tax and audit and consulting practices, he was caught in a whipsaw of conflicting goals and ambitions. He stepped down in March 1989. Although he claimed he was resigning because as a lame-duck CEO with only two years left to serve he could not lead the firm into a new era, the fact was that he was a victim of the kind of accounting-firm battle he had never dreamed he would see when he'd signed on as an Andersen auditor in 1954. Dramatic changes in the accounting profession put an abrupt end to his rule in the ninth year of his reign as Andersen's CEO.

Andersen was not alone in being buffeted by the winds of change. Much like Duane Kullberg, Arthur Young's chairman, William Gladstone, found his own consulting practice the target of an unsolicited bid by a former high-ranking MAS partner. The incident sprang from a dispute over the management of Young's consulting business.

"I was running the fastest-growing profit center at Arthur Young," said Al Beedie, formerly the firm's Midwest regional manager for consulting. "In seven years, from 1981 to 1988, our regional practice grew from about eighty people to more than four hundred, and we were continuing to grow by about fifty percent a year. In any well-run business, senior management would do whatever it took to sustain that growth, especially because it was the only really profitable part of the firm. But big accounting firms aren't well-run businesses. They're clumsy bureaucracies run by auditors who are protective of their power, who've been spoiled by a system that's assured them of a minimum level of fees over the years and who don't want to change. Period. That may be fine for them, but I knew that if I had to keep running my consulting division according to the auditors' rules, the growth we'd been experiencing would be history real fast."

Much as in the Andersen conflict, the gap in compensation between Arthur Young auditors and consultants became a sore point. As Beedie recruited and trained talented consultants, he found over and over again that they were lured away by independent firms offering two and three times the maximum salaries built into Arthur Young's pay scales. With Young's management insisting on virtual parity between its practice divisions, consultants' compensation had to remain roughly equivalent to that of the auditors.

"By the mid-1980s, it became increasingly difficult to complete searches for Arthur Young," said executive recruiter Stephen Page. "That's because the firm's salary structure was out of touch with the marketplace. They simply refused to pay the kind of salaries they needed to to attract high-level people. At the time AY's maximum consulting salaries were about $250,000, competing firms were paying $350,000. Faced with that kind of gap, we couldn't convince people to move to Arthur Young."

Although Beedie said he pressed firm management over and over again to liberalize the rules and allow him to offer competitive salaries, he claimed that Gladstone refused to budge. "I hired a guy as an MIS [Management Information Services] director for $95,000," he recalled. "Three years later, a competitor snapped him up with an offer of $300,000 a year. Another MIS guy I hired for $65,000 was lured away by a major corporation for $250,000. Half of the twenty-five partners working for me indicated that they would have to leave unless I could come close to the offers they were getting. But when I told firm management that I might lose up to fifteen partners in six months, their only response was that it was too bad and that I should go find other people."

Soon after this let-them-eat-cake encounter, Beedie pressed for a meeting between Gladstone and the Midwest consulting practice in early May 1988. Here, he says, he presented AY management with his master plan for the MAS department. Proclaiming that he could create a major new business for the firm, he asked for a separate framework for the MAS practice that would enable the consultants to set their own compensation structure and to formulate their own hiring policies. Although the unit would function more or less autonomously, AY would retain substantial equity in it.

"At the conclusion of my remarks," Beedie recalled, "I asked that the firm study these proposals to see if a separate organization could be established. At this point, Gladstone appeared to open the door to a more responsive policy, saying something like, 'Fine, we'll do a study.' But I knew Gladstone. When he didn't want to act on an idea, he launched a study and let the study kill it. So I pressed him, saying, 'If the study group agrees with our point of view, we'll proceed with the separate organization, right?' That's when he moved to dash our hopes, saying something like,

'Yeah, we'll do the study, but there's little likelihood we'll do what you want.' "

Convinced he could never build AY's MAS practice into a more formidable business, Beedie decided to leave the firm to launch his own consulting firm. But with a twist: In "secret" negotiations with a small group of his Arthur Young partners (senior members of the Midwest consulting practice), Beedie and the group planned to resign en masse, first making a $50 million bid for AY's Midwest consulting practice. A New York–based financing source, Butler Capital, was set to fund the deal.

But as the plan was being hatched—just days before the Beedie group was to make its offer to Young management— a mole in the ranks tipped off Gladstone, who promptly fired the "ringleaders," ultimately canning Beedie and his cohorts. By ridding the ranks of "troublemakers," management believed it was clearing the way for the great bulk of consultants to get back to work. But instead, they might have cast out one of the best executives in the firm.

"Al Beedie was a dynamo, a real charismatic guy who'd been extremely successful in building his practice," Stephen Page said. "Perhaps for that reason, the tax and audit partners never felt comfortable with him. And that's a shame. AY had a tremendous engine going in its information technology work. They were making a real impact in the marketplace until the compensation structure got in the way. From my perspective, they missed out on a wonderful opportunity."

In the aftermath of the dismissals at Andersen and Young, both firms found themselves embroiled in litigation with their former MAS partners. AY's suit charged a group of the Midwest regional partners with violating their partnership agreement by allegedly soliciting Young employees and clients for Technology Solutions, a new company formed by Beedie and a group of Arthur Young consultants.

"The partnership articles require that you devote your full-time efforts to the firm," said Carl Liggio, general counsel to Ernst & Young, the successor firm to Arthur Young. "Our discovery shows that Beedie was not doing that. What's more, we had contractual agreements with all parties in the firm saying, one, for a two-year period after leaving the firm, you will not solicit or serve those clients you served when at the firm, and, two, you will not solicit employees of the partnership for a similar period. Beyond this, there is a common-law principle that the partners of a partnership owe fiduciary obligations to their fellow partners and to the partnership. As Justice Cardozo said, 'There is no greater loyalty than a partner's to his fellow partners.' "

AY found this loyalty lacking and brought suit, seeking to collect damages of an unspecified sum. In retaliation, the former AY consultants countersued, seeking $15 million in damages. Grounds for the action involved AY's alleged efforts to block the successful formation of Technology Solutions.

"Arthur Young threatened Butler Capital, warning that if they financed our activities, they would be sued," Beedie said. "They also put the pressure on clients. Soon after we launched Technology Solutions, we got an assignment from Martin Marietta Corporation, which called us with the good news one afternoon at 3 P.M. But we had little time to celebrate. At 4:30, they called back to say the deal was off. Why? It seemed that Arthur Young had gotten to their legal department, threatening action if they hired us. Rather than risking litigation, they bailed out."

Even after AY launched its suit against Technology Solutions, the Beedie group sent the firm a letter, formally offering to buy its entire Midwest consulting practice for $50 million or to pay $30 million for a 20 percent interest. Almost immediately, Young rejected the offer. From that point on, the deal was dead.

For Arthur Andersen, whose consulting practice dwarfs Arthur Young's, the stakes were even bigger and the legal battle even more intense. The fireworks began after Brebach, joined by a number of former Andersen consultants, launched a new firm called Information Consulting Group. According to Andersen, which filed suit in January 1989, this was but the latest move in a plot to acquire its consulting practice. At the heart of Andersen's court case was the charge that Brebach's campaign against the noncompete clause had little to do with philosophy, ego or insult. It was, the litigation insisted, an effort to protect a secret plan to create an independent consulting practice staffed with Andersen defectors. The complaint alleged:

> During the winter of 1987 and the spring of 1988, Brebach, then head of Arthur Andersen's United States MIC [Management Information Consulting] practice, began working with Ross [Thomson Ross, a former member of Andersen's federal government information consulting unit] on more concrete "business plans" for an independent MIC practice and, in addition, began actively attempting to solicit and induce other MIC partners and practice personnel to join them in a commitment to separate all or large portions of the MIC practice from the rest of Arthur Andersen.

As the charges continued, certain Andersen consultants—allegedly acting as agents for Saatchi, Millar and Brebach—gathered small groups of partners to brief them on their "illicit plans to force a break with the MIC practice and thus acquire the building blocks for a new MIC practice in competition with Arthur Andersen."

This, Andersen alleged, was the real motive behind the April 1988 meeting at the "21" Club. Brebach's intention, the lawsuit charged, was to "solicit the participation of a key group of Arthur Andersen partners, representing the leadership of the MIC practice, to agree to abandon Arthur Andersen and join in the formation of an MIC practice in competition with Arthur Andersen."

Learning of Brebach's alleged goals, Andersen fired him on the grounds that he allegedly had violated "his fiduciary duties as a partner and a member of Arthur Andersen's senior management team." After leaving Andersen, Brebach allegedly kept the pressure on Andersen, inducing MIC partners and personnel to join the new firm, Information Consulting Group, which was financed by Saatchi & Saatchi to the tune of $20 million for working capital and another $10 million for an option to purchase the company by May 1990. Boiling down Andersen's charges to the bottom line, ICG was, they said, created not as an entrepreneurial venture for the firm's former consultants but instead as a stalking-horse through which Millar, Brebach and the other "defectors/defendants" could raid Andersen personnel.

But in a countersuit filed in the Cook County Circuit Court, ICG, Brebach and defectors named in the Andersen complaint told a dramatically different story, painting a picture of a troubled institution torn apart by the increasingly incompatible practices under its roof. Its complaint states:

Historically, members of the Audit Division have wielded the greatest amount of influence within the firm. The Consulting Division's increasing importance to Andersen's practice has not resulted in a corresponding increase in its influence. . . .

According to Brebach, once a break had been made with the launching of ICG, Andersen—very much a threatened giant—unleashed a reign of terror designed to quash the new firm. Allegedly, Andersen's tactics took three forms:

1 Making damaging statements about ICG, in that Andersen and its agents engaged in the most malicious mudslinging, falsely representing that an ICG principal would be going to jail for criminal activity; that other ICG founders had engaged in criminal wrongdoing; that ICG would not continue in business very long, its financial condition being such that it could last only six months; that employees of ICG would be left without jobs; that clients of ICG would be left with unfinished jobs when ICG went under; that ICG was an unethical company; that certain ICG principals had no morals and no business ethics. In addition, the complaint stated, *Andersen would do whatever it took to see that ICG never got a client* [author's italics].

2 Discouraging Andersen partners and employees from joining ICG by trying to intimidate prospective defectors, thus causing them to reconsider affiliating with ICG. The alleged campaign of intimidation included harassing telephone calls insinuating that the turncoats would be blackballed from the Big Eight. "They went as far as to threaten secretaries that if they as much as talked to us, they would be implicated in legal proceed-

ings," Brebach said. "Their goal was to create a climate of fear."

3 Pressuring prospective clients to refrain from doing business with ICG by warning them that working with the fledgling venture would put them at risk of litigation. "In one case," Brebach said, "a prospective client was so concerned about the legal repercussions of working with us that I had to bring our lawyer along to assure him that Andersen's case was baseless."

In summary, ICG's countersuit claimed that Arthur Andersen & Company—the billion-dollar-a-year behemoth of the consulting business—couldn't accept the fact that frustrated and dissatisfied partners would sever their ties with the mother firm and launch a business of their own. Allegedly angered, confused and threatened by this show of independence, Andersen had tried to suffocate the new venture at birth.

The battle of Andersen versus the defectors was a classic case of good versus evil. The question was, who were the good guys and who the outlaws? From Andersen's viewpoint, the defectors sought more than a career opportunity; they sought to steal their former employer's clients and consultants. To the defectors, Andersen was more than a professional practice seeking to guard its interests. It was a raging bully, determined to crucify a scapegoat rather than deal with the more challenging problems that were tearing the firm apart.

In the end, the litigation was settled in the summer of 1989 with all claims and charges dropped. As part of the settlement, ICG agreed not to hire Andersen personnel for a period of six months. To many, this was a clear-cut victory for ICG. "The fact is, Andersen never had a case," said David Lord. "Just about every court in the nation has sided with the right of employees to seek work elsewhere and the right of employers to come along and hire them. Andersen may have thought its lawsuit would have a chilling effect on ICG and other consultants contemplating similar spinoffs, but the suit actually had a more damaging impact on Andersen, showing just how vulnerable it felt by the formation of ICG. In hindsight, taking legal action was a stupid move."*

Whichever side you choose to believe, one thing is certain: The success of Andersen's MAS practice and the reluctance of the Andersen audit establishment to compensate its consulting peers monetarily and politically to the degree they believed they deserved created a climate in which conflict was inevitable. "Growth," Andersen's own partnership agreement notes, "creates an ever increasing problem of communication among the partners." And lack of communication breeds conflict, creating deep divisions in the ranks. Across the board in the big firms, as the balance of power shifts from the accountants to the consultants, struggle is inescapable, and there are no easy solutions, no obvious compromises. In such an environment, peaceful coexistence may be impossible.

The much-heralded reorganization that gave birth to Andersen Consulting was trumpeted by the firm's high command as an act of enlightened governance on a par with the Magna Charta. With this momentous step Andersen management claimed it had diffused a bitter rivalry, laid to rest a divisive feud, corrected inequities in the system and repositioned the firm to capitalize more than ever be-

* In October 1989, ICG was acquired by the prestigious consulting firm of McKinsey & Company, which bid for it at an auction set up by the Blackstone Group, a New York mergers-and-acquisitions boutique. The acquisition reflected McKinsey's determination to become a force in the systems integration business, a market long snubbed by McKinsey and its peers among the old-line "strategic planning" firms.

fore on the explosive growth in computer consulting. That claim was, in fact, more a hope than a reality. Although the consulting practice gained considerable power, the audit culture still dominated. Consider the fact that Kullberg's successor as CEO was none other than an up-from-the-ranks accountant, former chief operating officer Larry Weinbach.

A fast-tracker who joined Andersen after graduation from the Wharton School in 1961, Weinbach became a partner nine years later, at the age of thirty. At that time one of the firm's youngest partners, he hit pay dirt by specializing in the sophisticated accounting issues that were swirling around mergers and acquisitions. With the M&A market going through the roof, and with Andersen (like its peers among the giant CPA firms) seeking to capitalize on this lucrative niche, Weinbach's reputation as an M&A guru made him a highly prized member of the Andersen team. After a stint as assistant to the former CEO, Leonard Spacek, he continued to climb the ladder with stops along the way as PIC in Stamford, Connecticut, audit and accounting chief for the New York office (1980), head of the New York metropolitan office (1983), firmwide chief operating officer (1987) and, ultimately, CEO (1989).

Had Andersen been an ordinary firm passing through an ordinary transition, Weinbach would have been the ideal candidate to lead his troops into the last decade of the twentieth century. But Andersen is not an ordinary firm passing through an ordinary transition. In spite of the reorganization, Andersen is still a house divided. Beneath the surface, many of the auditors remain jealous over the consultants' role as the firm's new glamour boys and rainmakers.

On the other side of the DMZ, the consultants have won

some substantial victories. With the creation of AC, they have gained more autonomy over their operations and have won SEC approval to engage in joint ventures with Arthur Andersen's audit clients. But the consultants know that as much as things have changed, some have remained the same. Most important, they are still under the umbrella of an audit firm. Andersen Consulting's managing partner George Shaheen, for example, reports on a direct-line basis to Andersen's CEO, who remains the ultimate boss.

"In creating Andersen Consulting as a separate business unit," Victor Millar said recently, "Arthur Andersen has achieved a significant accomplishment that should give it an advantage in the Big Six. But this is not the end of the story. The evolution of the consulting practice will continue, to the extent that the organization they have put in place for the consulting practice now is not the same one you will see at the end of the decade."

Time may prove that the Andersen reorganization, complete with Kullberg's abdication, was little more than a truce, a cease-fire, a temporary lull in the fighting. Ultimately, increasing numbers of consultants are likely to want out of the accounting profession, cutting all ties to the CPAs.

"I think Arthur Andersen is preparing itself now for the day they don't have Andersen Consulting," Art Bowman said. "They've built up a tremendous small computer-consulting practice within the audit division, hiring hundreds of people capable of setting up turnkey systems for their clients. My money is betting that they're doing this at least in part with the anticipation that the problems dividing them will become too great to keep the consulting and auditing practices under the same umbrella. For example, should the need for investment capital exceed the consulting firm's ability to be adequately financed, I think we'll see the day when Andersen sells or otherwise spins off the practice."

Spinoffs will undoubtedly spread throughout the Big Six. As the march for independence becomes unstoppable, the firms will be forced to sell all or part of their consulting practices or risk the loss of those practices through open revolt. When that happens, the Big Six will have come full cycle, returning a century after their founding to their original station in life: They will be accounting firms.

4

IN HIS OWN
IMAGE

Mike Cook and the Remaking of
Deloitte Haskins & Sells

If any firm struggled valiantly over the years to retain the traditional posture of holier-than-thou professionals committed to the audit function, it was Deloitte Haskins & Sells. The seeds of the firm were planted in the late nineteenth century, when Charles Waldo Haskins, an accountant practicing in Brooklyn, and Elijah Watt Sells, a native of Muscatine, Iowa, served together on the Dockery Commission, a body appointed by Congress to recommend changes in the government's accounting system.

As a friendship developed between the two men, they decided to go into business together, and in 1895 they launched a small partnership. Six years later, Haskins & Sells moved beyond its home base in New York's financial district to christen a regional office in Chicago. From that point, growth came quickly. In 1905 a collaboration was formed with the British firm of Deloitte, Plender, Griffiths & Co.; during World War I, Haskins & Sells opened offices across the nation; and in 1919 the firm was hired by General Motors, which, seventy-two years later, is still a client. In 1978 the firm became known formally as Deloitte Haskins & Sells.

Over the decades, Deloitte joined the ranks of the Big Eight accounting firms, each with its own distinct culture and image. Deloitte became known as a stuffy, hidebound firm, committed to the "i"-dotting, "t"-crossing traditions of a Dickensian clerk. The white-shoe arrogance of Price Waterhouse, which considered itself the elite of the audit profession, was absent here. The Deloitte culture was concerned more with accuracy than with ego. When asked to describe themselves, Deloitte partners were proud to say, "We're the 'auditors' auditor.' " Technical proficiency was their trump card, and they used it to attract an impressive roster of solid, conservative clients who felt a kinship with Deloitte's bedrock approach to accounting and auditing. Signing on with the firm were such stalwarts of the U.S. corporate community as Dow Chemical, Procter & Gamble, Merrill Lynch and Monsanto.

In Deloitte's tight-vested environment, "business" was a dirty word. It was an article of faith to the men of the partnership—the first woman partner was not elected until 1974—that they were professionals practicing in a lifework as prestigious and scholarly as medicine or law. Yes, they were paid for their skills, but these were "fees" rather than salaries or commissions. And yes, they served client needs, but they were hired to fulfill "engagements" rather than just to do projects or jobs. Anything that smacked of commercialism was simply renamed, a euphemism put into its place.

"I remember calling the Deloitte partner who was responsible for our audit, suggesting that we meet for a 'business lunch,' " recalls a former corporate financial officer. "Well, you could just tell by the way the conversation screeched to a halt that the chap was repelled by the idea of a 'business lunch.' That was all right for insurance salesmen or textile manufacturers, but not for a Deloitte auditor. It was as if he couldn't imagine letting a client watch him eat. Barbaric. That's the way he reacted. As if the idea were barbaric.

"Instead, he suggested that we meet at one of those Ivy League university clubs that are headquartered in splendid brownstones in and around midtown Manhattan. It was either the Harvard Club or the Princeton Club or some such outpost of overgrown preppies. Anyway, holding court in a century-old leather chair in a century-old building, surrounded by century-old men who looked as if they were in a waiting room for the dead, that's where the Deloitte man fit in. Like a rumpled college professor at home on a makeshift campus."

As long as the audit practice continued to expand at a healthy pace, the Deloitte partners—like many of their peers in the Big Eight—could thumb their collective nose at the business marketplace and hold themselves aloof from the outright commercialism of sales, marketing and advertising. And why not? Everything was going their way. Clients still viewed audit relationships as long-term, if not permanent. Once clients signed on with Deloitte, they did so with the intention of staying with the firm for years, decades, generations. Fees, which the firm considered "annuities," were increased annually with hardly a murmur of protest. Competition, if it could be called that, was practiced with kid gloves.

"Let's say that in the old days Peat Marwick Mitchell

learned that one of our clients was unhappy with our performance for one reason or another," said Deloitte's current
chairman, Mike Cook, a hard-driving auditor–turned–
business-executive. "You might think Peat would view that
as a ripe opportunity to land a new client. But no, there'd
be none of that, not until Peat called and informed us that
we had an unhappy client that needed attention. The un-
written rule was that you didn't steal another firm's clients.
You might wind up with someone else's client, but only
after you gave the current auditor the chance to make good
with that company."

In every sense of the word, auditing was a gentleman's
profession. Men and women who knew from an early age
that they had no taste for the rough-and-tumble of corporate
politics, who abhorred the idea of selling themselves or
their company's widgets, turned to public accounting as a
safe harbor, a refuge. The best of them made it as Big Eight
partners, many with Deloitte. Here they could practice
accounting with little concern for the competition and pressures of business. Within the halls of the hallowed firms,
they were secure.

Or so they thought. But massive changes in the corporate
world put an end to that. It started in the 1970s as a new
generation of brash young CEOs came into power. Faced
with the growing threat of foreign competition, they put
performance before old school ties and, much to the con-
sternation of the giant accounting firms, they were willing
to trade off long-term audit relationships for lower fees.
Compounding this negative turn of events, the AICPA
lifted its ban on advertising and solicitation, allowing CPAs
to market their services openly for the first time.

Suddenly, competition had come to accounting. But the
Deloitte partners, accustomed as they were to a privileged
environment, hardly took notice of it. The facts that fees

were declining, that clients wanted more service for their dollar and that other firms would attack without a courtesy call were for the most part ignored. And why not? The way the Deloitte system was structured, its senior partners—who wielded most of the power in the firm—were completely insulated from the marketplace.

Lockstep compensation saw to that. Under this arrangement (which was more or less standard throughout the Big Eight), partners moved up the earnings ladder in tandem. Seniority drove the system. All of those making partner in a given year started off with identical earnings, and they were assured of nearly identical annual increases during their first five to ten years with the firm. Even after the elite in the ranks assumed management positions, the disparity in earnings was never great. That some partners were clearly superior to others in their peer group, that they were skilled practitioners or prolific rainmakers, made virtually no difference in the lockstep system. To find out how much money a Deloitte partner earned, one needed only to ask a single question: "How many years have you been with the firm?"

In such a cloistered environment, where fees flooded in and competition (if it could be called that) was conducted by the rules of etiquette, there was hardly reason to create a meritocracy. Replacing lockstep with merit-based earnings would only damage delicate egos, pit partner against partner and threaten the harmony of a collegial culture. As long as the practice remained robust, as long as things continued to go the firm's way, there was no reason to change.

Or was there? Once the marketplace began to change, once clients began to trim fees and demand more from their CPAs, Deloitte was slow to respond. All of the built-in factors that made life so pleasant for the senior part-

ners—the fraternal environment, the high lockstep earnings—blinded them to the harsh realities that were slowly
closing in.

At Deloitte, the winds of change began to blow in the
late 1970s, when, for the first time in the postwar period,
partner earnings—the key barometer of a professional
firm's performance—declined or failed to keep pace with
inflation. As events would prove, this was more than an
"off year"; partner earnings continued to drop (in real
terms) through the early 1980s.

By this time, the firm was quietly splitting into factions.
Suddenly, the same lockstep system that had assured internal peace for decades had become a source of conflict.
With the senior partners, all at the apex of the lockstep
pyramid, continuing to collect handsome earnings from a
shrinking pool of fees, the junior members of the firm saw
their earning power shrinking. Even more important, they
began to worry about Deloitte's future and about their place
in it. As young professionals in their thirties and early
forties, they would be inheriting the firm in the decade to
come. But what kind of firm would it be? Was the earnings
decline a sign of emerging problems? Was the firm poorly
positioned for the future? Would their earning power continue to shrink? For the first time in the firm's history,
there was concern for its fate. As the younger partners
gathered in small cliques, this concern was evident. And
it was just as evident that the elders in the firm were
oblivious to it.

It was at this point that Deloitte's fifty-seven-year-old
chairman, Charles Steele, began to anticipate his retirement, then five years away. With a changing of the guard
in the offing, Steele appointed a steering committee to

study the succession issue, including the replacement of much of the aging management team.

"As the succession study began," said Jon Katzenbach, a director with McKinsey & Company and a longtime consultant to Deloitte, "the firm's elder statesmen thought they had everything under control. Sure, earnings were down, but they assumed this to be temporary. As far as Steele and his team were concerned, the firm was in fine shape. Given a bit of succession planning, it would remain in fine shape for as far as anyone could see. But as they would soon discover, this optimistic view was hardly unanimous throughout the firm. What started out as a routine study would turn into a bombshell for top management."

Three leading partners—Pat Wade, PIC in New York, Bob Arnett, Midwest regional partner, and Mike Cook, then in charge of the Florida practice—were appointed to the steering committee.

Under the Deloitte system, which continues to this day, bright young partners from around the firm are handpicked to serve a two- to three-year tour of duty as the chairman's aide-de-camp. In this position, the aide functions at times as a secretary, taking minutes of important meetings, and at other times as an extension of the chairman, reprimanding partners in cases where the chairman prefers to let others be the bearer of bad tidings. Mike Cook, who had already served in this capacity, was considered as one of the most likely prospects to succeed Steele when the chairman retired.

Steele instructed Cook, Wade and Arnett to gather input on the succession issue, both by questioning the partnership and by gaining the advice of outside counsel. With this in mind, the group called on McKinsey's managing director, Ron Daniel, who suggested that Katzenbach—a senior partner with experience in organizing and managing large businesses—would be the right man for the Deloitte project.

"From the beginning," Katzenbach recalled, "I became a de facto member of the steering committee, interviewing partners along with Cook, Wade and Arnett. And it was together that we made a shocking discovery. The Deloitte partnership wasn't one big happy family. As we gathered input from the younger partners, it became clear that they were troubled. They told us in no uncertain terms that the firm had to look beyond succession to such fundamental issues as Deloitte's role in the Big Eight, its worldwide posture and its long-term plan. In a nutshell, we ran smack into a grass-roots outpouring of concern that took us completely by surprise."

As these long-simmering issues rose to the surface, it became apparent that the younger partners were troubled by the very cultural bias—Deloitte Haskins & Sells as the "auditors' auditor"—that the elder statesman wore as a badge of pride. No one was arguing that technical prowess in the audit process was a bad thing, just that it meant more to auditors than to clients. With corporate financial executives now viewing the Big Eight's audits as virtually identical, any claim of audit superiority fell on deaf ears. Increasingly, clients were interested in CPAs who could serve as business advisers, bringing a fresh perspective to their financial controls and to the totality of their operations.

At the leading-edge firms, auditors would identify problems or opportunities in client businesses, paving the way for their consulting brethren to develop related programs and strategies. But with Deloitte's myopic focus on auditing, the firm had one of the smallest MAS practices in the Big Eight. As a result, it was hard-pressed to serve the increasingly broad range of client needs.

As the younger partners viewed it, they were being held captive to the traditional emphasis on the audit. Because they recognized that greater growth and profitability were accruing to firms that had developed stronger consulting practices and adopted a more businesslike approach to the delivery of professional services, they wanted to reposition Deloitte to do the same.

"And they were on target, coming up with a strategy the firm sorely needed," Katzenbach said. "I remember speaking with a large banking client that was leaving Deloitte for Arthur Andersen. When I asked them for the reasons behind the shift, they said they needed help with revamping middle management information systems, the kind that Andersen was very good at installing. Deloitte said it could deliver a system of this type, but never did. They just didn't have the resources."

With major corporations beginning to favor the accounting firms with the strongest multinational practices, Deloitte's relative weakness on the international front was also of great concern to the forces of change in the firm. "I spoke to the president of a major money center bank that had just shifted its audit from Deloitte to Price Waterhouse," Katzenbach said. "It seemed the bank had just completed a major study of the international markets and found that DH&S was weak in the countries where they needed a strong accounting presence. Because of Deloitte's relatively poor position overseas, the banker also worried about the firm's ability to assure strong quality controls throughout the world. Summing it up, he said, 'There was just no way we could continue to work with them.'"

That there was a growing schism between the up-and-coming generation of Deloitte partners and the old guard was made evident by management's response to the emerging concern in the ranks: Considering it much ado about nothing, they wrote it off as the hysterical response of inexperienced partners. Even as the steering committee identified serious problems in the firm, Steele and his top lieutenants remained skeptical of the need to make fundamental changes.

This was where thirty-eight-year-old Mike Cook, until then Steele's obedient protégé, began to depart from his mentor. Gradually but undeniably, Cook's experience on the steering committee changed his perception of the firm. Starting off with a mind-set similar to Steele's—principally, that this was a healthy firm hardly in need of fundamental restructuring—Cook found that his exposure to concerned partners throughout the firm began to change his view of Deloitte. In time he became convinced that the younger partners were right. Sweeping changes had to be made, and the firm had to reexamine the way it conducted its practice and the way it responded to the changing market for accounting and consulting services. As a by-product of this personal transformation, Cook became a leader and a lightning rod for the younger partners, who began to view him as a champion of their cause. It was a constituency that would soon pole-vault him into the seat of power, over the objections of those who thought him too young and inexperienced to run the firm.

Working behind the scenes, Cook pressed Steele to extend the firmwide inquiry beyond issues of succession to the more difficult questions raised by the younger partners. At this point, working committees were established to investigate the principal components of the practice.

"Senior management still wasn't convinced that there was anything to the calls for substantive change," Katzenbach recalled, "but they were willing to continue with the fact-finding process to see what turned up. They said, take four months, speak to all of the partners, ask them to submit a written commentary on the issues within the firm and how they think these issues should be handled. Then report back to us. Their attitude was, 'We don't think there's anything here, but it's worth a look to find out.' "

The working committees were divided into four principal areas of study:

- *Market conditions:* Are major changes occurring in the marketplace? Have client needs changed? What do clients expect from their accounting/consulting firms? Does this differ from traditional requirements?
- *Competition:* Who are our competitors? Are they limited to Big Eight firms? Are the second-tier firms emerging as a competitive force? Should we be paying more attention to the independent consulting firms? In what direction are our competitors moving? Are we doing everything possible to remain competitive?
- *Firm economics:* Which of our services are most profitable, and which are the least so? Why are partner earnings failing to keep up with inflation, and what can be done to reverse this trend?
- *Organization:* Are we organized effectively? Can we respond well to changes in the marketplace? To clients' needs and demands? Are we set up to reward superior performance? If there are problems in our organization, what can be done to correct them?

The self-appraisal proved to be an exhausting emotional process culminating in an inescapable fact: Deloitte Haskins & Sells was a troubled firm. A declining power in the accounting hierarchy, it was in need of a massive reorganization—a top-to-bottom remaking of its internal systems, its methods of dealing with clients and competitors and its image in the corporate community. So sensitive were the findings that McKinsey memos referred to Deloitte by the code name LPF [Leading Professional Firm].

"Although they'd learned by this point that the partners had some genuine concerns," Katzenbach recalled, "the widespread conviction that drastic actions had to be taken took top management by surprise. They went into the process thinking their faith in the status quo would be confirmed, but they came out of it realizing they were badly mistaken.

"Fortunately, they didn't fight it. In fact, they became immediate converts to the need for change. That they did so, and that they recognized there was an urgency to this, proved to be a watershed for Deloitte because it gave the forces for change the opportunity to proceed beyond the study, using what they had discovered as a fulcrum for reshaping the organization in a way that could help it to retain its stature as a premier accounting firm."

As the venerable firm of Deloitte Haskins & Sells began the painful process of transforming itself into a modern, market-oriented firm, Mike Cook found himself at the vanguard of change. From the beginning of his career, he had been on the fast track, rising from a green auditor fresh out of the University of Florida in 1964 to firmwide director of accounting research in 1973 to Steele's aide-de-camp in 1978. His crowning achievement came in 1984, when he was elected managing partner, catapulted into that position by Charlie Steele.

Cook's rapid rise to the top was based on two factors: First, it was a classic case of the fair-haired boy turning a close relationship with the boss into a launch pad for his career. Ever since he had served as Steele's aide-de-camp, the bright, energetic Cook had impressed the chairman as a young man with the mettle to lead the firm. Second— and equally important—Steele perceived Cook's popularity with the new generation of partners and recognized that placating this group would be critical to the firm's stability once the current management team retired.

"It took guts for Charlie to appoint Mike when he did," Katzenbach said. "Many of the senior partners thought he was too young, that others were better qualified for the top spot. But Steele simply did what he thought should be done, and surprisingly, there was little flack over it."

It fell to Cook, as Deloitte's newly elected managing partner, to restructure the firm, to address and correct the concerns discovered throughout the painful process of self-appraisal. It was a job he relished. As an ambitious, aggressive man—a business manager in accountant's clothing—he welcomed the challenge of blowing the dust off a stodgy, dated institution and remodeling it in his own image.

In dragging Deloitte into the twentieth century, Cook employed what he called a series of "one percenters." Rather than attempting to reshape the firm with a broad-based assault on its old (and in some cases, cherished) traditions, he would adjust the delicate mechanism piece by piece. This was the height of diplomacy. When an institution is as old and as hidebound as the Deloitte Haskins & Sells of the early 1980s, change must be thoughtful, deliberate and prudent. Even those who appear to support reform wholeheartedly are put off by actions that seem impulsive and that ignore the time-honored preference for consensus-based decisions. By proceeding in piecemeal fashion, Cook knew, he could harness the enthusiasm of the younger generation without inciting a backlash from the old guard.

With a gusto and a tough-mindedness never before seen at Deloitte, Cook threw himself into the complex, politically sensitive job of transforming a venerable professional firm into a business. He did it first and foremost by scrapping lockstep compensation in favor of a meritocracy that rewarded partners for performance rather than seniority. He recognized that the compensation system was the key to unlocking the business potential trapped within the stuffy men's club Deloitte had become. If partners could count on automatic increases simply by surviving another year, if the bulk of the earnings was skewed to the oldest (and in many cases the least aggressive) partners, where was the incentive to perform, to attract and retain clients, to provide superior service?

"The compensation system was a natural first target for Mike's reforms, but it was also a terribly thorny issue," Katzenbach said. "That's because in a long-established professional firm, compensation becomes a sacred cow. The partners with the most power in the firm—generally the ones who've been there the longest—are the most determined to keep things just as they are. To bring about substantive change, you have to go head to head with the real forces in the practice. Mike was determined to do just that, and he had the support of the new generation to get it done."

Cook's first step was to demote seniority from the most heavily weighted component of Deloitte's compensation system to a minor factor accounting for no more than 10 percent of partner earnings. In place of lockstep compensation, he pushed through a complicated earnings formula

that weighed the partners' contributions in terms of their
management role (the stature of the clients they served or
the office they managed) and their professional performance (including rainmaking and client service).

A message was thus broadcast throughout the organization: You don't make money here by getting old. You
make money by bringing in clients, by serving them well
and by developing proficiency in marketable skills. This
deceptively simple message unleashed a wellspring of energy and ambition that until this point had been viewed as
a sign of impatience. For the first time, young partners had
an incentive to build up their practices, knowing that in
doing so they could outearn their brethren ten or twenty
years their senior.

"When I became a partner, it took me nine years to
reach the average of all partner earnings," Cook recalled.
"That's because under the old system, you had to endure
a slow, steady climb. But under the new compensation
system, a first-year partner could earn ninety percent of
average partner earnings and in the second year could reach
or even surpass the average. In the past we had failed to
motivate people to achieve their fullest potential. We told
people what we wanted them to do, but we didn't back it
up with money."

After Cook's reforms took hold, all that was ancient history. With a hoopla that would have made Messrs. Haskins
and Sells blanch, Cook passed out bonus checks to partners
bringing in major clients, to those landing engagements
carrying annual fees of $1 million or more and to those
successful in cross-selling consulting services to their audit
or tax clients. Although Cook was reluctant to label these
payments commissions (for fear of sounding unprofes-
sional), that was precisely what they were: monetary re-

wards for successfully selling Deloitte's services in the marketplace.

By tackling the sticky wicket of compensation and defeating the cultural bias that had long considered lockstep earnings sacrosanct, Cook commanded the attention of the partnership. From that moment on, it was clear to all factions in the firm that the managing partner was dead serious about effecting sweeping change and that he had the guns to make it happen. Those who read between the lines recognized that Cook's ultimate goal was to change Deloitte's self-image from that of a professional firm that happened to be in business (the traditional view among the giant CPA firms) to a business that happened to market professional services.

With that in mind, Cook extended his reforms to a set of practice components critical to profitability throughout the Big Eight:

- *Scope of services:* For the first time, Deloitte made a concerted effort to expand beyond the audit, bolstering its MAS division by establishing compensation incentives for building the practice and by recruiting senior personnel from outside the firm. Although Cook was not prepared to concede that the audit was a commodity like any other, he recognized that if partner earnings were to rise, high-margin services would have to be stirred into the pot.
- *Staff and partner utilization:* This critical benchmark of financial performance measures the percentage of working hours that can be billed to clients. In an efficient, productive environment, utilization hovers at around 80 percent. But at Deloitte, the percentage was barely 70.

Cook recognized that in firms as huge as Deloitte, the impact of greater utilization is enormous. With thousands of professionals boosting the number of hours they bill to clients, the bottom line grows in geometric proportion.

To boost utilization, Cook reversed a practice, then common throughout the Big Eight, whereby senior partners moved away from client service and into management of offices and headquarters departments. While this played to their egos, it transformed some of the best rainmakers in the firms from big fee producers to costly components of overhead. Committed as he was to a strong focus on client service, Cook forced many of these top partners out of their cushy jobs and onto the firing line, where they were obliged to generate fees. With each partner who returned to client work taking associates with him, this redeployment had a multiplier effect, substantially increasing revenues to the firm.

- *Leverage:* This yardstick measures the staff-to-partner ratio. Generally, the goal is to build leverage under the assumption that the more staffers there are on board and billing clients, the more the partners earn. But instead of building leverage, Deloitte had been building the partnership at a pace that had outstripped the growth in staff. Spoiled by years of uninterrupted growth and convinced that the Big Eight could defy the law of gravity, they had elected partners indiscriminately, rewarding the mediocre along with the exceptional on the theory that there would be money enough for all. But a growth in partners without a legitimate and corresponding increase in staff cuts deeply into leverage and, in turn, into profits per partner.

When Cook took the reins at Deloitte, staff-to-partner leverage was less than eight to one. If partner earnings were to rise, leverage would have to be juiced up substantially. To accomplish this, the old hands favored a sharp decrease in the election of new partners. And why not? That approach would protect the deadwood in the ranks—but at a very high cost. Rather than weeding out the least productive partners, it would force Deloitte's real future—the bright young managers waiting in line to become partners—to pay the price for streamlining a bloated, top-heavy firm.

More and more the businessman, Cook recognized that in limiting the slots for new partners, he would be cutting off the lifeblood of the firm. Unless young professionals could see a career path to partnership, unless they could aspire to the top positions, they would abandon Deloitte for other firms, other careers. This mass exodus of the brightest managers would severely damage the firm's recruiting abilities.

As much as he hated to admit it, Cook knew all too well that if he was going to succeed in creating a leaner, meaner, more businesslike firm, he would have to take the painful step of pruning back the partnership, in part by pressuring those who couldn't cut the mustard to take early retirement (prior to that decision, partners leaving a day before retirement age were ineligible for benefits).

"Identifying marginal partners and moving them out of the firm ran counter to the cherished notion of 'Once a partner, always a partner,' Katzenbach recalled. "So there was pain and some anger. But Mike was able to go against the grain of the Deloitte culture because of the strong support he had from the younger partners."

This Darwinian selection, which was proceeding simultaneously throughout most of the Big Eight, proved to be a watershed for the firms. Until that time, partnership had been more of a coronation than a job. Once admitted to the royal family, partners held their titles for life. Dismissal from the ranks occurred only in cases of alcoholism, mental incompetence or serious legal infraction. Barring such exceptional events, partners in the premier CPA firms, much like tenured university professors, were virtually untouchable. Their billable hours could nosedive, their professional skills could deteriorate to the point where they became embarrassments to themselves and their firms, but still they remained partners—blessed, thanks to lockstep compensation, with some of the biggest paychecks in the firm.

But with Cook's hardball decision to strip Deloitte of deadwood—and with similar purges under way at Peat Marwick, Touche Ross and others—the once-sacred concept of lifetime partnership fell victim to the increasing competitiveness and commercialization of the accounting profession.

"All of a sudden, the kind of partners that you would slide work papers to under their doors at 9 A.M., and they would slide them back to you at 5 P.M., were no longer desirable," said Jay Nisberg, a consultant specializing in the management of professional firms. "In their place, the firms wanted people who could go out and sell and market and make clients happy."

During all the years the Big Eight firms had enjoyed dramatic growth, they had been able to afford to be over-partnered. But once the growth slowed and the swollen ranks of partners had to compete for stagnant or, in some cases, declining profits, the rainmakers who were bringing in the big clients and charging out the maximum hours demanded they keep getting their due. In many cases, the only way to placate them was to force out the partners who weren't generating business. As tough as this was for the partners who were discarded, downsizing was essential. "No business can keep adding more and more mouths to feed," Katzenbach said, "when there's less and less food to feed them."

As Cook was busy reshaping the various components of Deloitte's practice, one thought occupied his mind: As long as auditors limited themselves to the traditional role of Dickensian bean counters, as long as they focused exclusively on clients' completed financial transactions, their services would be perceived as a necessary evil, required by securities laws but bringing little in the way of value added. The tendency to treat the audit as a commodity and to award engagements on the basis of lowball bids would accelerate. In the end, the profession would lose its status and prestige, forever forfeiting its ability to earn respectable fees.

With this in mind, Cook set out to change the auditors' mentality from that of backroom number crunchers to that of business advisers. "Based on their role as year-round auditors," Katzenbach said, "accounting firms had always been in a unique position to get into the bowels of their clients' operations and to offer management a fresh perspective on those operations. But they never capitalized on this. Why? Because they never considered themselves businessmen. They never thought like businessmen, and they never acted like businessmen, so how were they going to give clients a businessman's perspective?"

Cook thought he had the answer. He would do it by changing the way his partners thought. In meeting after meeting, in memo after memo, he stressed the need to go beyond the technical requirements of the annual audit and bring a fresh perspective to the clients' businesses. To reinforce this, he awarded the biggest bonuses and highest salaries to those who proved themselves capable of grad-

IN HIS OWN IMAGE

uating from being "auditors' auditors" to being business advisers.

From Cook's perspective, firms that had little to offer beyond a commodity service would find their fees being nickel-and-dimed to death by clients. But firms that could help clients solve problems or increase efficiency would be able to charge fairly for their work. And this, he was convinced, was a prerequisite of a strong, profitable practice. But just as Cook was reshaping Deloitte to match his vision of a professional firm as a lean, aggressive business, the rug was pulled out from under him.

In 1984, the same year Cook was elected managing partner, chairman Charlie Steele attended a series of secret meetings with Price Waterhouse chairman Joe Connor. The subject of discussion, then unprecedented in the Big Eight, was of a possible merger between the two firms. As Connor and Steele saw it, with one bold stroke they would create a giant among giants—a colossus of such size and prestige that it would gain a distinct advantage over the competition.

With the initial talks showing great promise, the two chairmen presented the proposed merger to their firms, each promoting the deal on the basis of international synergies and economies of scale. But beyond the grandiose statements, it was a case of empire building, with both men seizing an opportunity to crown their achievements. Steele, who was nearing retirement, would engineer the biggest deal in Deloitte's history, leaving behind a much larger firm than he had inherited. Connor, in turn, would be the reigning monarch of the world's biggest and arguably most prestigious accounting firm.

But there were hurdles to overcome. As the proud owners of the biggest salaries and egos in the Big Eight, Price Waterhouse partners wondered why they should allow mere mortals into their exclusive fraternity. To PW purists, the proposed name for the combined firm, "Price Waterhouse Deloitte," sounded more like a 1960s conglomerate than a professional firm. In a confidential memo to the partnership, PW's policy board admitted as much: "Emotional factors naturally enter into each partner's consideration of a merger of this magnitude. Many of us like Price Waterhouse the way it is, or the way it was when the partner group was smaller. These emotions cannot be minimized. . . ."

Meanwhile, inside Deloitte, where PW's arrogance was being experienced firsthand, the partners questioned if they could coexist with these raving egos. "We'd go into joint firm meetings to talk about the sharing of power, money and client responsibilities, but 'sharing' wasn't in the Price Waterhouse lexicon," recalled a senior Deloitte partner who attended more than a half dozen such powwows. "The PW guys had the script written before we got there. The way they saw it, the Price Waterhouse partners should make all the decisions. Our role was to nod our heads and take notes.

"But there was something even more pernicious than that, something the Price Waterhouse partners never said because they didn't have to. You could read it all over their faces. It was as if they were thinking, 'Do you guys realize how incredibly lucky you are to be merging with the great Price Waterhouse? You'd better hurry up and agree to the demands we're making, or we may change our minds and take back the offer to merge with you. Then where will you be?' "

With PW's high-and-mighty attitude ruffling feathers at

Deloitte, the initial betting was that there was little chance of a successful merger. But incredibly, the problem seemed to fade away. Whether the PW partners let some air out of their egos or the Deloitte partners learned to take PW arrogance with a grain of salt, things started to click. Suddenly, the vast majority of the partners in both firms got on the bandwagon in favor of a merger.

Mike Cook's position in all of this was interesting. Publicly, he supported the merger, demonstrating the loyalty he had always shown to Steele. But privately, he wondered why Deloitte should abandon the internal transformation that had been proceeding full steam ahead when the merger proposal surfaced. Excited by the opportunity to remake Deloitte in his own image, he feared that the merger would close the window on this initiative, and that his own plans (and ambitions) would be swallowed up in the combined firm.

"I felt strongly about leading the firm and putting in place the new strategies we were developing," Cook said. "But just as I got to the starting gate, someone said, 'We're not going to open the gate. We're going to do something different.' Naturally, there was some conflict on my part."

Put bluntly, Cook recognized that the merger could derail his career. Even though Steele assured his protégé that the Price Waterhouse partners were "our kind of people" and that Deloitte would benefit from PW's prestige and client base, Cook remained cool to the idea of a "Price Waterhouse Deloitte."

"Mike appeared to support the merger with Price Waterhouse, but never with the gusto for which he was known," said a former high-ranking member of the Deloitte team. "If the merger needed a cheerleader, he was content to let

Charlie Steele play that role. As a wise politician, shrewd beyond his years, Cook was careful to hedge his position.

"Mike recognized instinctively that if the merger failed to materialize, the senior partners most closely associated with it would be bloodied by the episode. That was a risk he didn't want to take. Fortunately for his sake, he didn't have to. With Charlie establishing himself as Mr. Merger, with the chairman willing to stake his credibility and his reputation on the transaction, Mike could stand in his shadow. If the deal failed, Mike could distance himself from it; if it proceeded, he could say he had supported it from the start."

Ultimately, this fence-straddling would turn out to be a brilliant move.

When the merger plan was presented to the Deloitte and Price partnerships for a vote, senior management turned up the pressure, warning their colleagues (as if they didn't know it already) that the Big Eight were competitive businesses locked in a numbers race, that the days of technical proficiency, of "auditors' auditors" and of professionalism as the hallmarks of a successful practice were long gone. Unless PW and Deloitte improved their rankings among the accounting giants, the partners were led to believe, they would face grave risks.

As PW noted in a report on the proposed merger:

> Internal growth is our present strategy. Notwithstanding our profitability to date, we may not have the necessary resources to keep pace with our larger competitors and to achieve our strategic goals in all aspects of our practice. In the past, PW's strategy has been to focus on our large client strength and to achieve high partner income. This strategy after World War II through the 1970's has left us resource

short for the competitive environment of the remainder of the decade, the 1990's and beyond. . . .

Any course of action, including this merger, has risks. Arguably our most significant risk would be to do nothing and run the risk that other firms will outstrip our capabilities in the future and perhaps require us to take actions which are strategically less desirable than merging with DH&S. . . .

The merger will not assure our future. Only our continuing efforts will do that. The merger will, however, allow Price Waterhouse Deloitte to realize its opportunities far better than either firm could realize them on its own.

With much fanfare, Connor and Steele signed a letter of intent on October 11, 1984, that called for a merger of the firms on the first day of the new year, subject to approval by the partners. But in spite of the optimism oozing from both camps, the deal soon came apart at the seams. In secret balloting tabulated by the law firms of Cravath Swaine & Moore (for PW) and Sullivan & Cromwell (for DH&S), the U.S. partnerships approved the merger, only to have the union vetoed by PW's powerful contingent in the United Kingdom.

In spite of months of deliberation, dozens of high-level meetings and expenses that ran into the millions of dollars, the first momentous merger of Big Eight firms was a bust, a nonevent. For Steele and Connor, the failure was a stunning defeat and a personal embarrassment. After warning their peers that each firm needed the other, the chairmen were forced to eat crow—an exercise in humility that Mike Cook was spared.

"Because Mike never made the merger his project, it never became his failure, either," said a highly placed par-

ticipant in the PW/Deloitte negotiations. "Instead, the fallout rained down on Charlie Steele. Licking his wounds,
he retired in 1986, at which time Mike succeeded him as
chairman."

The weeks following the stillbirth of Price Waterhouse
Deloitte were marked by anger, second-guessing and outright disgust. Feelings ran highest in the Deloitte camp,
where the partners felt betrayed, double-crossed and rejected by their counterparts at Price Waterhouse, whom
they had mistrusted from the start.

Now it seemed all too clear: They should never even
have talked with Price Waterhouse. Never shared sensitive
data with them. Never opened the books to the competition. Never accepted the idea that Deloitte—a proud firm
nearly a century old—should take second place in a merger,
seeing its great and glorious name trail that of Price Waterhouse like an afterthought, an appendage.

The hostility vented against Price Waterhouse was the
natural fallout of a marriage that comes apart at the altar.
To work for months planning every detail of the merger,
to swallow personal and professional pride, to start thinking
of oneself as a partner in Price Waterhouse Deloitte, to do
all this only to have the groom walk away—for whatever
reason—was galling. Insulting. Outrageous.

Compounding this wounded pride, a deep sense of confusion and bewilderment gripped the Deloitte partners.
For a year the firm had looked inside itself, going through
the painful, often torturous process of admitting its own
weaknesses and taking dramatic steps to correct them. But
with the start of the Price Waterhouse negotiations, this
internal reshaping had been postponed as the partners focused on the logistics of a megamerger, a merger that would

spell the end of their firm as an independent entity. Now that they were back on their own, where would they turn? Would the firm be the Deloitte of old, or would the commercialization launched under Mike Cook pick up where it had left off?

Here Cook's shrewd strategy of maintaining some distance from the merger worked to his—and the firm's—advantage. Because he had never been the merger cheerleader, because his greatest enthusiasm had been reserved for the remaking of Deloitte as an independent firm, he could lead the move back in that direction, spurring the partners to complete the process that had shown such promise before the merger became an issue.

"I thought that once the merger was called off, the momentum for change within Deloitte would have dissipated," Katzenbach recalled. "After all that had taken place, I didn't think there'd be any taste for reform. And it might have been that way were it not for Mike Cook. But that's a big 'if.' Mike simply refused to let the momentum die. Like a single-minded crusader, he pushed and pushed and pushed to get the process going again."

Revealing a shrewd instinct for leadership, Cook used the failure of the merger, and the bitter taste it left with his partners, as a rallying point for continuing to update and modernize Deloitte. If they don't want us, the message went, then it's just too bad for them. We're not going to back away with our tails between our legs. We're going to be tougher and smarter and more aggressive competitors than ever before. To hell with Price Waterhouse. To hell with the rest of our competitors. We're going to take them all on—and we're going to win!

How to implement this get-tough policy, though, was a question mark. Some of the partners urged Cook to snatch victory from the jaws of defeat by arranging a shotgun merger with another Big Eight firm, a proposal Cook jumped all over. "After the Price Waterhouse vote came up negative," he said, "the fundamentals that drove the merger talks were still there. A strategic combination with the right Big Eight firm continued to make sense for all the reasons it had made sense at the start. But we couldn't explore this approach again, not for some time. You can't keep telling your partners and clients, 'We're going to merge,' only to have that merger come to naught. Do that, and soon enough you'll appear desperate, as if you can't make it on your own."

Weeks after the Price Waterhouse merger was called off, the managing partners of two Big Eight firms called Cook to explore mergers. As a courtesy he met them for lunch, but without any serious interest in pursuing this approach. Rekindling merger talks would create an air of uncertainty about Deloitte Haskins & Sells, and as Cook knew only too well, for a professional firm uncertainty is devastating. After singing the praises of the merger to partners and clients, Deloitte had to assure both groups that the firm could be vital on its own. With this in mind, Cook came out fighting.

After the merger collapsed, Cook immediately launched into the remaking of Deloitte, installing his much-heralded performance-based compensation plan, trimming the partnership (mostly by "encouraging" the deadwood to take early retirement) and closing down marginal offices that had never lived up to their expectations or had failed to achieve sufficient profits. Taken together, these steps made for a much-needed and long-overdue housekeeping, a sweeping out of generations of procedural cobwebs from a sleepy and once out-of-touch practice. With the internal system modernized and streamlined—and thus capable of rewarding energy and innovation (as opposed to seniority) —Cook began to rewrite the book on Deloitte's marketing tactics.

Historically, the Big Eight had done little or nothing to market their services. And for decades, they hadn't had to. Throughout the long period of sustained growth, business had seemed to materialize out of thin air. Blessed with the prestigious imprimaturs, firms like Price Waterhouse, Haskins & Sells and Arthur Young had been pursued by America's industrial sector. "Marketing," the partners joked, "is a matter of picking up the phone when it rings."

By the time Cook moved into the chairman's office, however, the inside jokes had turned to serious discussions about marketing, salesmanship and all the other business skills the firms had failed to master over the years only to find they were now critical for attracting and retaining clients. Here, more aggressive competitors like Touche Ross, Arthur Andersen and Coopers & Lybrand had a head start, all having introduced a range of marketing tactics in the late seventies and early eighties. These new tactics had been designed to sharpen the practice focus and direct resources to the fastest-growing and most lucrative markets for professional services. In an age of specialization, the firms recognized that clients were beginning to hire professionals less on the basis of old school ties and more on the basis of specialized expertise.

It was with this in mind that Cook began to direct Deloitte's human and financial resources to high-profile target industries. Traditionally, the firm had made equal investments in about twenty-five practice segments, without regard for growth or profitability. In those days, its practice had been a mile wide and an inch thick. But when Cook took over, he narrowed the focus to five growth industries that deserved the greatest resource allocation: public utilities, financial institutions, real estate, health care and manufacturing.

Cook's niche marketing strategy helped to transform Deloitte from a dated practice weak in the fastest-growing disciplines to a firm that became the first choice of some of the business community's most sought-after clients. This was most evident in the leveraged buyout, mergers-and-acquisitions arena—a market that in the late 1980s was as white-hot for DH&S as it was for Wall Street.

Deloitte's ties to the LBO market dated back to 1976, when the firm had been hired by the newly launched Kohlberg, Kravis & Roberts. When KKR emerged as the preeminent practitioner of leveraged buyouts and one of the most successful of the new breed of Wall Street deal makers, Deloitte (which had had ties to the principals during their previous association at Bear Stearns) clung to its coattails, earning a reputation as knowledgeable advisers in the field. For that reason, such clients as Wesray Capital and the Blackstone Group joined the Deloitte fold. In one fell swoop, a firm long considered a relic of the past became known as a savvy financial adviser capable of satisfying the sharpest, most demanding minds on Wall Street.

If Deloitte Haskins & Sells hadn't had a Mike Cook, it would have had to invent one. His special skill was in the ability to camouflage his hard-driving businessman's mentality in the framework of a cautious, conservative CPA. From the beginning, he was embraced by his partners because he appeared to be one of them: a dues-paying member of the audit fraternity.

Because he carried himself with the drip-dry demeanor of a bean counter, and because he was enough of a diplomat to coax reform through the organization rather than bulldozing over the partnership, he breathed life into the De-loitte culture without stirring up great controversy or conflict. As managing partner and later chairman, he accomplished a difficult feat, bending the firm to his will while still appearing to be consensus-driven and faithfully reflecting the goals of his partners.

What made his performance so extraordinary was that in his heart of hearts, Cook thought like an autocrat. What was good for Mike Cook, he assumed, was good for Deloitte Haskins & Sells. "I'm a big fan of Mike's—I think he's done a heck of a job for Deloitte—but he runs it as if it were his firm rather than the partners' firm," said Art Bowman, editor of *Bowman's Accounting Report*. "What Mike Cook wants, Mike Cook gets."

In the final analysis, a managing partner's popularity is tied to the figures on the bottom line. Profits are the litmus test of his performance. When the firm prospers, he is a saint; when partner incomes decline, he is the living embodiment of Murphy's Law: a CPA who has risen to his level of incompetence. That Cook rose to become chairman was further testament to his popularity, but much of the support he enjoyed came as a direct result of the good numbers he posted on the board. During his tenure, Deloitte has moved from the bottom of the pack in financial performance to high rankings in these key benchmarks (figures are pre-merger, 1989):

- Fees per partner soared from $586,000 to $1.05 million.
- Profits per partner rose sharply from $143,000 to $240,000.
- Tax-practice fees mushroomed from $92 million to $222 million.
- Staff per partner (the key to high leverage) grew from 7.5 to 1 to 8.4 to 1.

- The audit practice expanded by 77 percent, from $309 million to $547 million.

But for all the improvement in Deloitte's culture and its operating statistics, ominous flaws continued to haunt the practice even after Cook's business strategies were incorporated into the firm. The chairman fell short of his goal of making Deloitte a power in the fast-growing, high-profit practice of management advisory services, a failure that can be traced, in part, to the low profile Deloitte had in the market long before Cook planted his flag atop the firm.

But in spite of the problems he inherited when he took command of Deloitte, Cook had to take part of the blame for the failure to make the firm's name synonymous with consulting as well as with accounting and auditing. In fact, his own shortcomings played more of a role than he would have cared to admit. "Mike has done good things for his firm, but he's far from a perfect managing partner," said a confidant who has worked with Cook since his days as Charlie Steele's heir apparent. "He's stubborn and single-minded, and he tends to talk more than he listens. When he decides that something should be done in a certain way, that's the way he does it: right, wrong or indifferent.

"From my standpoint, that's why management consulting has fallen short of his expectations. When he first started talking about building up the consulting practice, I suggested that he fire about one third of the MAS people and then go out and hire a core group of about eight top people from outside the firm. People with skills and smarts and rainmaking ability. People he could build a big new practice around.

"But my words fell on deaf ears. Mike had it in his mind that the people already in place could fix things up. Even though it was clear to many of us that he was working with a weak group, he refused to consider other options. Things would proceed the way Mike Cook thought they should proceed because he's bullheaded and that's the way bull-headed managers operate."

With consulting's growth eclipsing that of accounting and auditing, Deloitte found itself in a vulnerable position. Yes, partner earnings, utilization, leverage and all the other key indicators of financial performance were up, but the firm's ability to serve the increasingly broad, complex consulting requirements of its bedrock clients remained an ominous question mark, one that might lead to the loss of a trophy client on the order of a Procter & Gamble, Merrill Lynch or, heaven forbid, General Motors.

Another threat to Deloitte's future stemmed from the fact that it had remained relatively small by Big Eight standards. As much as Cook had turned Deloitte's sluggish numbers around, it was still near the bottom of the rankings; its largest competitors, Arther Andersen and Peat Marwick, were about twice its size. Despite bursts of brag-gadocio touting Deloitte's performance under his com-mand, Cook harbored a fear that the giant firms could be split into two tiers, with the two behemoths, Arthur Andersen and Peat Marwick, all alone at the top and Deloitte somewhere down below. Were that to happen, clients might view Peat and Andersen as being in a class by them-selves, giving them immediate access to more and more of the most sought-after engagements.

From Cook's perspective, the threat of overpowering competition would assume crisis proportions if members of the Big Eight were to begin to merge, thus creating a new class of superfirm. The way he saw it, a single merger would be likely to ignite a chain reaction in which all the firms would scurry for partners. In this game of musical chairs, Cook's worst nightmare was to be left without a seat.

In an address to Deloitte's international partners in Munich in October 1988, Cook told those assembled that he felt no immediate pressure to merge. But then he warned them about "externally driven changes in our competitive environment that would cause us to change direction." One of those "externally driven changes" came with a jolt on May 19, 1989, when Ernst & Whinney and Arthur Young announced they would merge, thus creating the largest accounting firm in the world. From that moment on, Mike Cook recognized that the Big Eight would no longer exist— and that Deloitte Haskins & Sells could not continue as an independent firm.

5

BYE-BYE, BIG
EIGHT

The End of an Era

To desire immortality is to desire the eternal perpetuation of a great mistake.

—ARTHUR SCHOPENHAUER, *THE WORLD AS WILL AND IDEA*

News of the Ernst & Young merger confirmed everyone's suspicions that a Big Eight megamerger was bound to occur. Ever since Price Waterhouse and Deloitte Haskins & Sells had raised the specter of a marriage between the giants, all of the firms' managing partners had been obsessed with the idea of lining up a potential mate. In secret meetings at Chicago's Ritz-Carlton and New York's Pierre Hotel and the "21" Club, cliques of senior partners met with their counterparts, sparking an endless stream of rumors that Deloitte would merge with Arthur Young, Young with Coopers, Coopers with Touche, Price with Young, Peat with Deloitte, Young with Ernst & Whinney.

The reason for this prolonged mating dance was clear: At least two years before Ernst & Young broke the ice, the firms had recognized that they had to consolidate. Two major factors contributed to their thinking. First, to have a major presence in the United States, each practice needed about a hundred offices. With corporate America doing business in the top one hundred cities, the top accounting firms had to be similarly located. But this meant a huge overhead. The office rental costs alone were staggering.

Second, technology had become a significant cost factor. When auditors had visited clients in the old days, they'd taken little more with them than a few pencils and a calculator. But as they upgraded to computers and workstations, their costs increased dramatically. "Faced with this surging overhead," said Touche Ross's former chairman Grant Gregory, "management started to think in terms of consolidation and the economies of scale that would yield. That's when all eyes turned to mergers. We knew they were coming. The only questions were when and with whom."

Given the clash of cultures that would be the inevitable by-product of a intra–Big Eight merger, most of the rumored combinations were implausible if not impossible. But there was one exception: From the beginning, the rumor joining Arthur Young and Ernst & Whinney had made all the sense in the world.

Culturally, the firms were kindred spirits. Both were at the stodgy end of the practice curve, both still prided themselves on being auditors and both had a fortress mentality that made them among the most secretive of the Big Eight. Even more important, the proposed merger offered synergies that promised to fill in the weak spots in both practices.

From Ernst & Whinney's perspective, Arthur Young's international organization would add muscle to the firm's overseas network, just as global capabilities were looming as the key to winning some of the most hotly contested engagements. But if a merger would be beneficial for Ernst

& Whinney, it would be a godsend for Arthur Young. E&W's $1.3 billion in U.S. revenues would bootstrap AY, which had been generating about $900 million in revenues, from the sixth position to number one among the big firms. Considering that the Big Eight were locked in a numbers race—with all of the firms striving to improve their ranking in the accounting hierarchy—this was bound to be a welcome move.

But in Arthur Young's case, there was even more at stake. In virtually every key performance measurement, AY ranked below E&W. According to *Bowman's Accounting Report*, the firms stacked up this way in 1989:

	ARTHUR YOUNG	ERNST & WHINNEY
Average billing rate	$70 per hour	$82 per hour
Hours charged per professional	1,465	1,566
Utilization	70.4%	75.3%

On the bottom line, AY partners earned an average of less than $200,000 a year, or $70,000 less than their E&W counterparts. For a Big Eight firm touted as one of the most prestigious in the profession, those were unhappy numbers, ranking AY below many firms a fraction of its size.

"When we saw the numbers for Arthur Young, we were shocked," said the managing partner of a prominent mid-sized firm based in New York. "Our partners earned more than theirs, and we never had access to the giant engagements they inherited simply by being a Big Eight firm. Judging by their dismal performance, we had to conclude that they were a poorly managed firm."

Although the tight-lipped Young partners would have

been the last to admit it, the firm worried about falling behind its peers. There was widespread fear of a scenario that was preoccupying senior management: that the firm would tumble to last place in the rankings, falling behind the faster-growing Deloitte and Touche, which held the seventh and eighth spots respectively. In this lowly position, Young partners (like their peers at Deloitte) saw themselves being overwhelmed by giants Arthur Andersen and Peat Marwick.

At one point, *Bowman's Accounting Report* ran a piece saying that if the firms' respective growth rates continued, Arthur Young could wind up in eighth place, behind Touche Ross. Some weeks after the story was published, editor Art Bowman called Young's chairman, Bill Gladstone, about another matter, only to find that he refused to take the call. Thinking at first that he was just busy, Bowman returned the call several times, but to no avail.

"That's when I knew he was avoiding me, but as to why that would be, I hadn't a clue," Bowman recalled. "So I called another source at the firm to ask what they knew about it. What they told me came as a shock. It seemed that Gladstone had taken umbrage at my story about Young's lowly position in the Big Eight—so much so that he wasn't going to talk to me anymore. And if that wasn't enough, he was canceling the firm's subscription to my newsletter. No doubt any hint of Arthur Young sliding to the bottom of the Big Eight had hit a nerve."

Clearly, the merger with Ernst & Whinney would prevent that and propel an edgy and sensitive Arthur Young to the top of the rankings. For both AY and E&W, the union would bring many sought-after benefits. But as they soon discovered, it also brought waves of chaos to the once stable and orderly firms.

Even before the merger was consummated, power plays

erupted as the partners in charge of practice offices around the country struggled to retain their posts and headquarters executives positioned themselves for dominance over their new rivals for the top spots. With careers on the line, questions echoed throughout the halls of AY and E&W: Who would run the newly merged Chicago practice, the partner in charge of Ernst & Whinney's Chicago office or his counterpart at Arthur Young? Similarly, who would run Los Angeles, Dallas, San Francisco? And who would head the industry practices in real estate, banking and manufacturing? The new firm was to be called Ernst & Young, a testament to the fact that E&W would have the upper hand in most matters. Nevertheless, disagreements flared over hundreds of issues. During this turbulent period, nothing worked well.

To wit: A major Midwest-based consumer products company was in the process of inviting the big firms to bid for its audit when the news broke that Arthur Young and Ernst & Whinney were merging. At that point, the company didn't know where the new firm would be headquartered. Would they use Arthur Young's headquarters in New York or Ernst & Whinney's main office in Cleveland? This was important because the company's audit director wanted to make sure that a letter asking the firm to bid was delivered to the appropriate location.

To find out, he called Arthur Young's New York offices, asking where the merged firm's headquarters would be. The telephone operator had no idea what he was talking about—it seemed as if no one had bothered to tell her about the merger—so she connected him with human resources. But it was no better there. The human resources person acted as if he were speaking a foreign language. Either she too was in the dark about the merger, or she didn't know where the firm would be headquartered. In either case, the prospective client wasn't gaining much confidence in Ernst & Young's ability to perform the audit.

"Still I persisted, stating again that I was with a major corporation that was interested in having the firm compete for our audit, and that all I needed was a proper address," the audit director recalled. "That's when the person on the other end asked, 'Is that all you want to know?' Relieved, thinking she had the answer after all, I said, 'Yes, that's all I need to know.' With that, she promptly hung up on me. That was my introduction to a megamerger."

Behind the scenes, the parties to the amalgamation of Ernst & Young recognized that it was more of an acquisition than a merger. The fact was that Ernst & Whinney had eaten up its smaller, more vulnerable rival. In issue after issue, conflict after conflict, Ernst & Whinney held sway, dictating the terms of the union.

Nowhere was this more evident than the terms of the secret profit split that would give E&W's partners 65 percent of the merged firm's profits for the first three years, with the remaining 35 percent going to AY's partners. Considering that E&W's partners had outearned their AY counterparts by about $70,000 in 1989, that seemed only fair. But given both firms' penchant for secrecy and their curious conviction that they were immune from the First Amendment, they tried to stop *Bowman's Accounting Report* from publishing an internal memo revealing the profit split. Although *Bowman's* ultimately prevailed in court, the extent to which the firms would go to shield the details of the merger revealed what can happen to sensitive egos when giant firms combine.

In another highly sensitive issue—one that would rear its head after the merger was consummated—the merged firm was forced to choose between two of its trophy clients,

Coca-Cola (an E&W client) and PepsiCo (an AY client). Ultimately, the decision was made to go with Coke. Although this was justified in terms of dollars and cents— Coke paid about $5 million more in annual fees ($14 million versus $9 million)—its position as E&W's pet client since the 1920s was the swing factor in siding with Coke. Behind the mask of excuses, it was another case of E&W pulling rank, a move that would infuriate critics of the profession, who viewed it as a shocking case of client influence on an "independent" accounting firm. At the same time, it would rile the former AY partners, who had long prided themselves on being Pepsi's auditors and who had to look on helplessly as the engagement went to Peat Marwick.

In spite of the turmoil the merger brought to the houses of Ernst and Young, it was seen as only a temporary disruption. Of greater consequence was that the union created a more powerful firm, the largest in the world, and that this combination effectively ended the era of the Big Eight. With the familiar oligopoly no longer in existence, E&Y's competitors rushed to forge alliances of their own. Just weeks after E&W and AY partners voted on June 22, 1989, to approve a merger, four other Big Eight firms announced that they too were planning to merge: Price Waterhouse was exploring a union with Arthur Andersen, and Deloitte Haskins & Sells would combine with Touche Ross.

From the outset, the Price/Andersen match had little chance of succeeding. Yes, the combination would be formidable, pairing the elite client base of Price Waterhouse with the cool efficiency and consulting expertise of Arthur Andersen. On paper, it would be the only Big Eight merger, real or rumored, to result in a combined entity truly greater than the sum of its parts. The merged firm would be at once the largest and the most prestigious in the profession.

No one knew this better than Andersen's senior management, which for more than a decade had considered the concept of a Big Eight to be obsolete. From Andersen's perspective, there were actually a Big Four and a Lesser Four. The former included Andersen, Price Waterhouse, Peat Marwick and Coopers & Lybrand. The latter—Ernst & Whinney, Deloitte, Arthur Young and Touche Ross— were viewed as second-rate competitors, more of an occasional nuisance than a real threat in the hunt for major clients.

By joining forces with Price Waterhouse, the Andersen people believed, the combined entity would occupy the top position in the highest echelon of firms. Few would argue with them. Although the competition wasn't talking for the record, there was more truth here than they cared to admit. Many had long feared a merger between PW and Andersen.

Behind the scenes, the two firms had made eyes at each other for some time. Whenever Andersen's Larry Weinbach and PW's senior partner Shaun O'Malley had bumped into each other at professional functions, they had shared the latest rumors about who was merging with whom and what those mergers might mean to their respective firms. Occasionally, they had kicked around the idea of merging, but the talks had always been hypothetical. Neither was particularly interested. "But that changed soon after Ernst & Young and Deloitte and Touche announced that they were merging," O'Malley recalled. "It was then that Larry called me from Europe, suggesting that we get together immediately. From that point on, the discussions began in earnest."

On the surface, the would-be merger appeared to have everything going for it: size, clout, prestige and profits. But as knowledgeable observers could see from the beginning, the strengths both firms brought to the table would turn on them in merger negotiations, rising as a formidable obstacle that neither side could scale. After decades of viewing themselves as the cream of the Big Eight and competing with each other in a long series of hotly contested engagements, PW and Andersen found it difficult to compromise, to accept the other side's point of view, to take a backseat on any but the most banal matters.

Adding to these ego battles, a number of substantive issues divided the firms. In the critical area of retirement compensation, a huge gap separated PW's partners, who were earning about $100,000 a year at retirement, and Andersen's retirees, who were collecting a paltry $30,000 annually in their senior years. Just how to level this out was the subject of considerable debate. PW had no intention of "lowering itself" to Andersen's level, while Andersen worried that PW's unfunded liability would "put a strain on the combined firm." From Andersen's perspective, the cost of covering PW's retirement liability was the deal killer. Considering PW's nine hundred active partners and the ranks of its retired partners (all assured a hefty retirement check), Andersen felt the liability it would have to assume was too great to justify.

For Price Waterhouse, the real thorn in the side proved to be Andersen's consulting practice. With Andersen Consulting having emerged as a formidable power in its own right, PW's much smaller MAS practice feared it would be dominated by the colossus from Chicago. And PW's auditors, who were jealously guarding their blue-chip audit clients, feared potential conflicts with Andersen's consulting practice. Specifically, PW auditors worried that the

SEC rule forbidding CPA firms to engage in joint ventures with their audit clients would force them to relinquish IBM and other prestigious computer-industry clients. "If I sent out a message to our clients that we were focusing our efforts on consulting, I'd be sending out a negative signal about auditing that didn't reflect our thinking in any way," O'Malley said. "I wasn't about to do that."

To PW's great frustration, the firm's negotiating team found itself across the table from not one but two parties, Arthur Andersen and Andersen Consulting, each with a different perspective. In the end, PW and AC found they could not coexist. When push came to shove, PW was unwilling to jeopardize the audit relationships that had traditionally assured it the highest fees and the greatest prestige of the Big Eight. Conversely, Andersen's consultants, flexing the muscles of their newfound semiautonomy, were intent on pursuing their mission of broad-ranged business advisers and joint venturers. From O'Malley's perspective, this was the real merger buster. "The Andersen Consulting guys didn't look me in the eye and say, 'We don't want this deal to be done,' O'Malley said. "But they did look me in the eye and say, 'We want to pursue our own goals, our own mission.'"

Even if the consultants had been willing to compromise, the timing of the merger was poor. Weinbach and O'Malley were both new at their jobs, and both of them wanted more time to put their internal programs into effect before dealing with a merger. Also, Andersen had just come through a trying period, having negotiated a truce between its auditors and consultants. That truce hadn't been tested yet. What's more, with Peat Marwick having merged with Klynveld Main Goerdler (KMG), and with Arthur Young and Ernst & Whinney and Deloitte and Touche merging too, O'Malley and Weinbach feared that the Justice Department might say "Enough!" and close the door on additional mergers. The last thing either man wanted was to do a deal only to find out it would have to be undone. "In the end we realized that we would be better off ending the negotiations rather than trying to force through a merger that wasn't meant to be," O'Malley recalled.

Weinbach also knew it was time to throw in the towel. "After three months of discussions, we had to make a decision on whether to merge or not," he said. "With a partnership meeting coming up in October, I didn't want to tell my partners that we were still talking—that there was nothing new to report. When you can't agree after talking and talking and talking, that becomes a message in itself. And the message was that this merger was a dead issue."

To Art Bowman of *Bowman's Accounting Report*, the prospect of Price and Andersen tying the knot was "a joke from the start."

"Think about it. On one side of the table, you had the Andersen faction assuming that the new firm should be called Arthur Andersen; on the other side you had the PW clan, thinking that the new firm should be called Price Waterhouse. Hell, these guys couldn't even agree on a name. Both went to talks with unrealistic expectations. Andersen hoped to acquire an audit practice and Price hoped to acquire a consulting practice. But trade-offs like this don't just happen in huge firms like that—not when the parties are too taken with themselves to strike a deal."

Such was not the case with Deloitte Haskins & Sells and Touche Ross. While an Andersen–Price Waterhouse union might have been a marriage of convenience, the merger of Deloitte and Touche was a matter of necessity.

Whereas PW and Andersen were cocky and secure in

their single state, Touche and Deloitte were frightened and weak-kneed. Both worried that their lowly positions in the pecking order threatened their status should a new clique of superfirms emerge.

For Touche Ross, being in the eighth position among the eight firms that dominated the accounting profession had always been a sore point, but one it could live with. Just having that Big Eight membership card made it eligible for all kinds of business that wouldn't come its way were it number nine or ten. So as much as it dreamed of growing to the point where it could surpass a Coopers or an Ernst & Whinney and thus finally look down on others the way everyone else looked down on it, it could accept life as the runt of the Big Eight.

But that acceptance changed dramatically with the emergence of Ernst & Young and speculation that another and even more concentrated combination of giant firms might replace the power and prestige of the Big Eight. Were membership in a Big Six or a Big Four to become the benchmark of the accounting elite, and were Wall Street underwriters to instruct their clients to get a "Big Four opinion" as a seal of approval, Touche Ross, no longer part of the elite, would have to scrounge for business like every other mere mortal firm.

"That prospect scared the bejesus out of the partners," said a former Touche Ross practice executive. "They knew that should that happen, their earnings would take a serious drubbing."

A similar fear spread through the Deloitte camp, where the partners had already endured an ego-bruising merger experience with Price Waterhouse and where there was little appetite for a new courtship. But as painful as that might be, Mike Cook recognized that he too could not allow his firm to fall outside the exclusive fraternity of the world's largest accounting and consulting firms.

The more Cook pondered the problem, the more he saw it in terms of client relationships, particularly the impact it would have on Deloitte's proud position as the long-term auditors of General Motors. If a Big Eight firm's identity were ever built around a single relationship, Deloitte's association with the auto king came closest. "Firms of our size are often judged by the premier corporations we represent," Cook said. "And when it comes to premier corporations, General Motors is one of the crown jewels."

Ever since Haskins & Sells had landed GM in 1918, the engagement had renewed itself with the predictability of Detroit's model-year hoopla. Over the decades, only the highest-ranking partners had qualified to lead the GM engagement, and Deloitte's chairman traditionally served as ambassador to General Motors, attending the car manufacturer's board meetings and acting as a senior adviser to GM management on broad-based accounting and auditing issues.

As Mike Cook looked out toward the horizon, playing worst-case scenario with Deloitte's future, he could foresee a set of events leading to GM's decision to "take a fresh look" at its audit relationship. Knowing full well that a loss of this magnitude would reverse the momentum he had brought to Deloitte—and, equally important for an image-conscious chief executive, that it would mar his tenure as chairman—Cook was determined to take any step necessary to preserve the GM relationship. Most important was to keep Deloitte from slipping from the ranks of the world's leading accounting firms. Given its relative weakness overseas and in the consulting arena, only a megamerger could assure that.

Throughout the late 1980s, Deloitte partners had explored the possibility of joining forces with virtually all its peer firms, most notably Arthur Young, Ernst & Whinney and Coopers & Lybrand. A merger with Price Waterhouse had been shot down only at the last minute. From a historical perspective, Young and Whinney would have been the most likely merger partners, both having come from a similar tradition of tight-vested practitioners proud of their heritage as auditors and slow to tip the scales in favor of consulting. But now Young and Whinney had become Ernst & Young.

At the other end of the spectrum, Touche Ross appeared to be the least compatible with Deloitte. As the youngest of the Big Eight (founded in 1947) and the most opportunistic, Touche had a hip, slightly irreverent culture that often clashed with those of its peers among the accounting giants. For decades after its founding, Touche remained the black sheep of the Big Eight. When the traditionalists at Whinney or Young or Deloitte grumbled about declining professionalism, it was Touche Ross they would point their fingers at. But times had changed. With all the firms desperate for merger partners, even Touche and Deloitte were willing to entertain thoughts of holy matrimony.

The first serious discussions took place when Mike Cook and Touche chairman Ed Kangas met to "compare notes" on the general subject of mergers. As the two men talked, they recognized that the historical differences that had long separated Deloitte and Touche had narrowed in the waves of reform that had changed both firms. Under Cook, Deloitte had been transformed from a hidebound relic of another era into a performance-driven enterprise scaling new heights in fees, profits and productivity. In the same years, Touche—which had always been business-minded—shed some of the excesses that had tainted its image and began to focus more and more on quality and professionalism.

In short, Cook and Kangas found that their firms were more alike than anyone would have guessed. What was more, the chairmen themselves agreed on a critical point: To survive and prosper into the twenty-first century, they were convinced, accountants would have to conduct themselves "as businessmen who happened to be professionals."

Much like Deloitte, Touche Ross had suffered through a wrenching period of change in the 1980s. The turbulence had begun when the popular and highly successful managing partner Rus Palmer—who had led Touche to a 237 percent increase in fees during his ten-year term—left the domestic firm in 1982 to head the international firm and then became the dean of the Wharton School. Convinced that one man alone could not fill Palmer's shoes, the partners elected a duet to run the firm. The way the organization chart spelled it out, fifty-two-year-old auditor Dave Moxlee would be chief administrator, running the firm day to day, while forty-three-year-old auditor-turned-rainmaker Grant Gregory would oversee client relationships, with the emphasis on bringing in new business.

From the start, this awkward arrangement was doomed to failure. First, Moxlee and Gregory were polar opposites. The former, a play-it-by-the-book accountant, was an old-fashioned, soft-spoken, self-effacing gentleman, conservative in style and substance. Gregory, on the other hand, was a skilled, flamboyant salesman. In a relationship that required a consensus-style approach to firm governance, the men could hardly agree on anything. Decisions that Palmer once had made in the course of a ten-minute meeting would drag on and on with both men taking different stands or—just as bad—refusing to take any stand at all.

As the partners took stock of the paralysis that was gripping Touche, some singled out Gregory as the heavy, pointing to what they considered to be a mightier-than-thou attitude. As a former Touche partner now with a midsize New York practice, recalled, "Perfect example: When he spoke at one of the partners' meetings, he had a big video screen mounted on the stage. The official reason was that we'd be able to see him better, but the way I sized it up, he wanted to create the impression that God was speaking."

But in all fairness, Gregory's mandate was to add clients and fees to the Touche Ross partnership and keep the firm from falling into the abyss of a second-class (or sub–Big Eight) practice. Partners who complained that Gregory was aloof and arrogant were missing the point. The way Touche was structured during his tenure, hand-holding was not his job. If the partners had concerns, insecurities, complaints—all of that actually fell into Moxlee's bailiwick. As Mr. Outside to Moxlee's Mr. Inside, Gregory's mission was to keep current clients content with Touche Ross and to bring major new business into the firm. If partner earnings declined (in real terms) during this period, Gregory argued, this was to be expected.

"It's one of those 'damned if you do, damned if you don't' situations," he said. "That's because no one can achieve the dual mandates of increasing practice growth and quality while simultaneously increasing earnings. The investments you have to make to achieve the former don't pay off until years down the road. The partners may not have looked at the big picture, but I had to. And that's all right. As the head of the firm, I didn't expect seven hundred people to see the world as I saw it. Instead, I had to pursue the goals I was elected to achieve, recognizing, as Franklin Roosevelt said, that this is 'the risk of leadership.' "

Gregory's experience as a leader of a Big Eight firm illustrated the bind managing partners can find themselves in. Just as corporate CEOs must respond to shareholder expectations of rising profits and stock prices, Big Eight chairmen must satisfy the partners' appetite for steadily increasing earnings. This calls for a delicate balance: Management must make sufficient investments to assure the firm's continued strength and competitive position without undermining the quest for ever-higher earnings.

Clearly, many in the Touche partnership felt that Gregory and Moxlee had failed to achieve this balance. Perhaps it was the fault of the awkward management structure that had sought to replace dynamic, decisive Rus Palmer with a two-headed armadillo. Perhaps it was Moxlee's conservatism or Gregory's aggressiveness. Whatever the cause, after three years of joint leadership the partners were ready for a change.

Under the Touche system, the top men served for three-year terms after which they stood for reelection to another three-year term, to a maximum of three terms or nine years in office. Until the Gregory/Moxlee reign, reelection had been pretty much a formality. Never in the firm's modern history had a managing partner been voted out before his maximum term was over. But in 1985 there was widespread sentiment that Grant and Moxlee had to go. Partners felt the firm was floundering and that they had to clean house and install new management to get Touche moving again.

The decision came out as part of an internal Touche appraisal conducted near the end of the managing partners' term in office. At the time, a questionnaire was sent around to the partners, asking if they thought things were going well or if there should be a change in leadership. As they stated in their letters and in personal appearances before the firm's nominating committee, the partners felt that Touche had stopped dead in its tracks and that it was time for a change at the top.

When the Touche partners voted for new management in 1985, they returned to the tried-and-true tradition of one-man rule. It was decided that responsibility for running the firm would be vested in the managing partner (as had been the case during Rus Palmer's tenure) and that Ed Kangas, then national director of Touche's profitable consulting practice, would be the best man to assume the top spot. Although Gregory could stay on as chairman, he would be second in command to Kangas, and he would have to stand for reelection after each one-year term.

According to a partner close to both men, when it became clear that Gregory would have to relinquish the reins, Kangas apparently hastened his exit. "Once it was apparent that Grant could no longer run the firm and that Kangas would succeed him, the question was what Grant would do," said the former Touche partner. "From what I understand, Kangas told him to take as much time as he needed, but to find someplace else to go. Ed didn't want him hanging around as chairman, even if that position was now subordinate to the managing partner.

"Being the shrewd political animal that he is, Ed never let this appear to be a one-on-one confrontation. He was too shrewd for that. Why get into hand-to-hand combat with the man he was replacing? Instead, he lined up powerful allies and used them as leverage in his talks with Gregory. Rather than saying, 'I've decided this or that,' he would say, 'My management team has decided . . .' How could Grant argue with that show of force? Although he could have stayed on with the firm, it would have meant going back to a practice office. For a man who'd run the show, that would be anathema. So after serving for about a year as chairman under the new setup, he resigned."

Gregory, who insisted that he left on his own volition, having planned to retire early from the start, later became a merchant banker with the firm of Gregory and Hoenemeyer.

On September 1, 1985, Ed Kangas assumed power as managing partner of Touche. A former auditor who had risen to head up the Midwest consulting practice before being appointed national MAS director by Rus Palmer in 1980, Kangas's rise to power followed the modern Touche Ross pattern. In much the same way as a gregarious and charming Rus Palmer had moved up the partnership ladder, reaching down for Grant Gregory as he rose rung by rung, so too had a gregarious and charming Gregory sponsored Kangas.

"No doubt Grant served as Ed's rabbi, lifting him through the ranks as he was moving ever higher," said a former Touche principal. "In fact, Grant was instrumental in getting Palmer to appoint Ed as the firm's consulting chief. I'm not saying Ed Kangas wouldn't have made it on his own—certainly he's smart enough to—but in a firm like Touche where there are hundreds of stars, having an ally at the top is invaluable. It pulls you out of the ranks of promising prospects and makes you the heir apparent."

But in this case, the protégé soon began to upstage his mentor. Midway through his tenure, Gregory looked back to find Kangas ready to occupy the chief executive's office before the incumbent was ready to leave. With Touche's earnings flat, and with the partners grumbling about the current leadership, Kangas—who had made a name for himself by taking MAS fees from $28 million to more than $100 million—emerged as the ideal candidate to turn Touche around.

His entrepreneurial quality appealed to the partners. In one of his favorite spiels, he talked about "building a money tree." The way he explained it, this was done by treating clients well and by cross-selling the firm's services to them. "I remember a particular presentation he'd put on, revealing how he'd turned a modest client relationship into a cash cow that generated fees of twenty times the initial billings," the former principal recalled. "Consultants could always come in and tell us how to build our practices, but Ed was different. Because he'd done it himself, he had great credibility."

As Kangas took over the reins, he initiated a series of moves designed to rejuvenate Touche, to reverse the trend in partner earnings (which had declined in real terms) and, in turn, to prop up sagging morale. He began (as had Mike Cook at Deloitte) by cutting the fat out of the partnership, trimming the ranks by more than 350 employees—half by normal attrition and half by handing out pink slips to mediocre performers. To Kangas this streamlining was a matter of good business; to the victims of the purge, it was ruthless.

A former member of Touche's small-business practice recalled his expulsion from the ranks when he failed to generate minimum fee levels: "When it became clear that I would fall short of the mark, those partners appointed as the unofficial Touche Ross henchmen started pressuring me to leave. The white-collar goons let it be known in no uncertain terms that my former partners, my good buddies in the Touche Ross 'family,' wanted me out. Technically, they needed a vote of the partnership to kick me out, but faced with the prospect that I was no longer wanted there, I just left. When you're shown the door by the people you used to call your partners, the only thing you can salvage is your self-respect. If they take you out kicking and screaming, you've lost that too."

The dismissal of partners from Touche, Deloitte, Peat Marwick and others was another indication of how much accounting had become a business like any other business— and how the big-firm partners were really employees masquerading as members of a higher calling. The fact is, there is nothing more noble or pristine about an accounting firm partner than about a corporate marketing manager or an account executive at an advertising agency. To grow in their respective organizations, to gain perks and bonuses and promotions, they must contribute in some meaningful way to the bottom line.

Although this realization came as a shock to those who had been indoctrinated in the benefits of a fraternal culture, the new breed of managing partners recognized that to dwell in the past was to forgo the future. In the increasingly competitive environment, with clients placing the emphasis on performance rather than mystique, there was no other option. If partners had to be fired, so be it. If salesmanship had to be a critical part of the culture, so be it. If trust and compassion and tenure had to give way to bottom-line performance standards, so be it.

At Touche Ross, Kangas forged ahead with a three-point business plan for turning the firm around. In addition to cutting away the deadwood, he reduced overhead by closing offices and dismissing support staff, consolidated staff functions and boosted revenues, in part by ending the firm's penchant for lowballing. The results spoke for themselves. From 1985 to 1989, Touche posted the following numbers:

- Partnership earnings up 86 percent, from $113 million to $210 million
- Revenue per professional up from $84,000 to $129,500
- Revenue per partner up from $622,000 to slightly less than $1.1 million
- Earnings per partner up from $138,000 to $245,000
- Total U.S. revenues up from $511 million to $925 million

By mid-1989, the Touche Ross turnaround had propelled the firm to the high end of the performance charts, making it among the most profitable—measured on the basis of net income per partner—and fastest-growing firms of the accounting elite. Judging by the charts and statistics alone, Touche was in excellent shape, its business-minded practice well positioned for the new realities of the marketplace.

But there was more (or less) here than first met the eye. Beneath the veneer of success, Touche was plagued with an ominous problem. Beyond its own client base, it had a relatively poor reputation. In a survey of one thousand chief financial officers conducted by *Bowman's Accounting Report*, those responding ranked Touche lowest among its peers in terms of "nonclient perception" of the firms.

To an aggressive business builder like Kangas, this was the worst of all handicaps. While he could drive the partners to leverage existing clients by cross-selling audit, tax and consulting services, in the greater universe of prospective clients, Touche was at a serious disadvantage. In part because of the firm's messy management brouhahas, and in part because it had always been perceived as a maverick operating outside the accounting establishment, the Touche Ross name didn't sit well with many corporate executives in a position to hire accountants and consultants. All too often, when Touche proposed for new business, the firm was knocked out of the box on the basis of its image alone.

"When you go out to win new business and the people in a position to hire you think of your firm as schlock city, it's darn hard to get that new business," said Art Bowman. "That was Touche's problem. They had a whole bunch of negatives—including a weak culture and a tattered image. While Touche's competitors could always rely on the prestige of their premier audit clients to rub off on them, Touche was very weak in that department. They audited only about twenty-five of the *Fortune* 500 companies— hardly enough prestige to offset the problems they had."

Much like Deloitte's Mike Cook, who was holding court less than a mile away on Manhattan's West Side, Ed Kangas recognized that in spite of Touche's sharply improved statistics and outward signs of success, the firm was in dire need of a merger. The reasons were compelling:

- Cursed with a poor image, management needed to white-wash the Touche Ross name by associating with a more prestigious firm.
- Were Touche to remain independent in the face of Big Eight mergers, it would likely fall into a less prestigious category of secondary firms.
- With international practice becoming increasingly important for gaining and maintaining clients, Touche recognized that it had a dangerous weakness, one that would have to be addressed if the firm was to remain competitive with its stronger peers.

When they looked closely at Europe, both Touche and Deloitte recognized that they were vulnerable in critical markets where they simply could not afford to be. For example, Touche's weakness in Germany made it susceptible to client losses there. By the same token, Deloitte's paltry presence in Japan was a glaring weakness in its international practice.

That the big CPA firms had to bolster their presence overseas was hardly a new concept. There had been talk about it for years. But suddenly the future had arrived. By the late 1980s, big business was operating in a one-world framework. With the globalization of the financial markets and with computerized communications linking corporate operations around the world, the multinationals were now truly multinational. To match their global presence, they wanted CPA firms capable of providing strong, cohesive services worldwide. Because it was weak on a global basis, Touche was being excluded from some of the biggest, most prestigious audit engagements. The message was ominous: "We don't think you have what it takes to play in this game."

Adding up all the negatives, Touche Ross was in more desperate need of a merger than any of its peers. With its bottom-rung ranking and last-on-the-list image, it was the least equipped to go it alone as an independent CPA firm. So when Ernst & Whinney and Arthur Young announced they were merging, Ed Kangas knew the time for talking, exploring and playing "what if" had come to an end. He would have to find a merger partner posthaste, a goal that had suddenly gained the same sense of urgency for Mike Cook.

The initial contact between the two firms was made on an athletic field in New Canaan, Connecticut. Soon after the Ernst & Young merger was announced, Kangas went to watch his son play in a lacrosse game. It was there that he ran into a neighbor, Bill Parrett, who was running Deloitte's Stamford office. With both of their sons active in sports, Kangas and Parrett had often met on the sidelines, shooting the breeze and cheering the boys on.

"At first it seemed only natural to see Bill at the lacrosse game," Kangas recalled. "That was until I remembered his sons didn't play lacrosse. During the course of the game, Bill approached me, saying, 'We know you guys have been thinking about a merger, and you know we've been thinking about the same thing. So why don't we get down to it?'

"To which I replied, 'Why don't we?' "

That this was an idea whose time had come was evidenced by the speed with which the parties moved from a sports field to a signed contract. The day after the lacrosse encounter, Parrett arranged a meeting between Cook and Kangas. In less than a week, the managing partners held the first secret powwow in a suite at New York's Waldorf-Astoria, a neutral site roughly equidistant from their respective offices. Cook opened the session by handing Kangas a printed statement declaring that the only mergers that work are mergers among equals—a simple but brilliant gesture that set the tone for a harmonious accord.

This one tête-à-tête was all it took for both men to see that a deal could be done. Because this would be a merger of equals in fact as well as in theory, neither Cook nor Kangas would have to convince their partners to swallow their collective pride. And because both firms recognized the need to merge, they were open to compromise. Within ten days of their first meeting, Cook and Kangas held two more top secret sessions at the New York Hilton. Here, the two senior executives hammered out a framework for the new firm, including the question of who would hold the power, an issue that was a sensitive one for Mike Cook.

"I got along fine with Cook until I printed something that said, in effect, that his ego would prompt him to demand the top spot in any merger," said Art Bowman. "From what I understand, he got bent out of shape on that. His people called to tell me he was pissed off. The following month, I ran a piece about a merger document rumored to be circulating between Deloitte and Touche. Cook denied it. But a Deloitte staffer I quoted said that a merger was in the offing only if Mike Cook could be in charge of the merged firm. I heard from his people that he was ticked off at that one too."

Ultimately, diplomacy held sway, and it was decided that with the merger Cook would assume leadership of the domestic practice while Kangas claimed control of global operations. That they could work to iron out this and other issues so quickly and effectively was testimony to the fact that both were strong-willed, decisive men blessed with a talent for perceiving a goal and surmounting obstacles in pursuit of it. While their counterparts at Price Waterhouse and Arthur Andersen had focused on the barriers to a merger and in the process allowed those barriers to achieve impregnable status, Cook and Kangas set their sites on a larger, stronger firm and were determined to achieve that objective. With both sides bringing this "can-do" perspective to the negotiating table, barriers collapsed in their path.

But a shared vision wasn't the only factor that drove the managing partners to work quickly. With the Ernst & Young merger igniting the long-awaited chain reaction of proposed (or rumored) combinations among the other firms, Cook and Kangas (much like Weinbach and O'Malley) feared that the Justice Department's antitrust division would turn their thumbs down on future megamergers. Sensing they had a narrow window of opportunity to structure a deal, Cook and Kangas moved with great dispatch, presenting their partners with a fully detailed merger package ready for a vote. Approval by both partnerships came on August 11, 1989, and it heralded a new era: The Big Eight had become the Big Six.

In spite of the hype that pictured the Deloitte and Touche merger as a synergistic marvel that created a stronger, more competitive practice, the firms had merged not so much to capitalize on opportunities but to ensure their survival as the accounting oligopoly shrank into a smaller group of Goliaths.

Even a longtime Deloitte adviser and confidant saw the merger as a shortcut that merely circumvented the firms' real problems. "When the firms merged," he said, "they justified the move by claiming they could eliminate duplication in their operations. But I was skeptical from the beginning. CPAs aren't very good at taking costs out of their practices. If anything, they keep building them in, building them in. And as to the 'synergistic fit,' as they liked to call it, I didn't think they had the management skills to bring that off."

On still another front, Mike Cook argued that in merging with Touche Ross, Deloitte was adding substantially to its MAS capability. But critics responded that while he was getting more MAS people, he wasn't building a cohesive MAS practice. "If Mike wanted to beef up his consulting capabilities," said one well-placed observer, "he should have gone out and bought a consulting firm that fit more closely with Deloitte's own strategy. Instead, he was forced to weld together two firms that really didn't belong under the same roof.

"When this happens, management spends all of its time trying to put the beasts together. The focus shifts from client service to the mechanics, the power plays, the ego-tistical tug-of-wars involved in making a merger work. All too often, the managing partners go into these deals thinking they'll be great, only to find they're saddled with an enormous array of problems."

From the beginning, more than mere problems haunted the merger of Deloitte and Touche, starting with minor foul-ups and snowballing into a near disaster. Shortly after the announcement that Deloitte & Touche would be the newest accounting megafirm, Cook led a new business team on a visit to one of the world's premier consumer products companies. In a ritual that was becoming all too familiar to the accounting giants, the corporation was taking a "fresh look" at its auditor relationship and inviting proposals from all of the Big Six.

Eager for a crack at this prominent, highly lucrative client engagement, the firms submitted "statements of qualifications" outlining their resources and capabilities and then scheduled appointments to meet with the corporation's financial staff. In the dog and pony shows that followed, a bevy of managing partners made personal appearances. Playing the role of elder statesmen, they pressed the flesh and sought to charm the prospective client. Mike Cook, who relished this role, was usually good at it. But even he couldn't stop the joint Deloitte-Touche pitch from turning into a fiasco.

"Although the merger had just been announced," said one of the corporation's senior financial executives, "the Deloitte-and-Touche contingent made a concerted effort to present themselves as one firm, already as solid as a rock. But much as they tried to create that impression, an invisible line split them down the middle.

"On one side, the Deloitte guys were uniformly impressive, speaking intelligently and fielding questions with authority. But on the Touche side, it was a different story. When their partners answered questions, they seemed to be tentative, uncertain, ill prepared. All in all, you got the feeling they were in over their heads—so much so that my people were embarrassed just watching the Touche performance. And we weren't alone. By the way the Deloitte team squirmed in their seats, you could tell they were mortified."

As if the Touche contingent hadn't done enough to repel the prospective client, Mike Cook sealed the firm's fate with what for him was an uncharacteristic faux pas. Informed that Deloitte & Touche had been cut from the list of auditor candidates, Cook refused to accept the decision diplomatically. The pressure to make the merger work may have distorted his good sense. "When I told Cook that his firm had been eliminated from consideration as our auditors, he asked why," the client executive recalled. "Being perfectly frank with him, I said that we had been impressed with the Deloitte team but that the Touche partners appeared to be poorly qualified for an audit of this magnitude.

" 'Oh, don't worry about that,' Cook said, 'I can just replace the people you met. We'll get new personnel for the engagement.'

"Still, I told him that I was sorry, but we had narrowed the field to three candidates and Deloitte & Touche wasn't one of them. That's when Cook pressed on, refusing to take no for an answer. He had the gall to ask if he could go over my head and take his case to our CFO. I wasn't going to argue with him, so I said, 'Sure, go ahead.' But let me tell you, I was furious. Not because I thought my decision would be reversed, but because the authority vested in me was being questioned. 'It would be a great understatement to say that Mike Cook failed to endear himself to me."

Instead of viewing foul-ups of this sort as a bad omen, or as a sign that Deloitte and Touche were incompatible, Cook and Kangas forged ahead. For the merger to succeed, they knew, they would need near-unanimous support from the overseas practices, which would operate under the banner of Deloitte Ross Tohmatsu (DRT). (Tohmatsu, originally Touche's Japanese affiliate, was a power in the important Tokyo market.) Self-confident salesmen that they are, both men believed that they would have little trouble selling the deal worldwide. Yes, there had been pockets of resistance from the start, but once the worldwide practices understood the big picture (as drawn by none other than Cook and Kangas), the managing partners were certain they would fall in line.

But the plan began to unravel shortly after the U.S. partners blessed the merger. It was then that Deloitte's big British firm declared that it would not join Deloitte Ross Tohmatsu and instead would link up with Coopers & Lybrand in the United Kingdom, ultimately to create Coopers & Lybrand Deloitte. In short order, Deloitte's Dutch firm, Deloitte Dijker Van Dien, followed suit, abandoning DRT in favor of Coopers. Before the architects of the merger could absorb what was happening, two critical components of Deloitte Ross Tohmatsu were out of the picture, both preferring to go to the competition rather than to merge with Touche Ross, a firm they were convinced would detract from their stature in their own domestic markets.

"Deloitte's U.K. practice—which was blessed with more than its share of big, prominent clients—always had this high-and-mighty attitude, sort of the way Price Waterhouse views itself in the U.S.," said a key participant in the creation of Deloitte & Touche. "Perched on this pedestal, they looked down on Touche Ross in part because it was smaller and in part because it had a downscale client base. So when the Deloitte snobs were asked to merge with this rather pedestrian group of fellows, to them it was like Rolls-Royce being asked to joint-venture with Hyundai. Heaven forbid."

None of this came as a real surprise to Cook, who had heard rumblings in the ranks from the first hint of a merger with Touche Ross. Given the defection by firms that would have been key members of Deloitte Ross Tohmatsu, it was a wonder he stormed ahead as if all of his troops were still in line.

"No way I'd do a deal where two or three of the principal firms in our practice didn't want to go along," said Coopers & Lybrand's blunt-talking chairman, Peter Scanlon. "I'd have had it screwed down before the merger was announced, or I wouldn't have proceeded. No way I would risk blowing Coopers & Lybrand apart for some perceived benefit. No way I would put some of our major professional associations at risk. My partners would throw me out of here if I did that."

Although Cook disclaimed any prior knowledge that the U.K. firm might defect, there was reason to believe he was so hell-bent on consummating a merger in light of the successful union of Ernst & Young (and the proposed betrothal of Price Waterhouse and Arthur Andersen, which was then still under discussion) that he rushed to consummate the deal, counting on his powers of persuasion to keep the would-be defectors in the fold.

"When the split came, Mike flew back and forth between New York and London, trying desperately to mend the rift," said an observer familiar with Cook's version of shuttle diplomacy. "He made several impassioned pleas to Deloitte's U.K. firm to buy into the merger, but regardless of what he said or what he offered, there was no changing their minds."

A former senior partner with Deloitte's U.K. practice added this comment: "It's a mystery to me why Mike Cook acted the way he did regarding the Touche Ross merger. Our resistance to that wasn't something that just cropped up. We had talked about merger prospects for two years. We said we favored a merger for the critical mass it would give us on a global basis—we even submitted the names of firms we would look favorably on merging with—but we made it clear all along that Touche Ross was not one of those candidates. At the end, we tried to get Mike to forge a union with Coopers, but he said he was too committed to Touche Ross. Mike thinks he's a good salesman. But a good salesman must listen to his clients, and Mike didn't listen to us."

In short, Cook had a disaster on his hands, an especially embarrassing disaster for a man who up to this point had prided himself on having a tight grip on his firm. For the first time since he had come to power, he felt impotent, unable to control the course of events.

Compounding the problems facing Cook and Kangas, Deloitte's U.K. partners took Deloitte Ross Tohmatsu to court, suing to prevent the newly merged firm from using the Deloitte name, which had originated more than a century earlier in the British practice. Ultimately, the court ruled in favor of Deloitte U.K. and barred Deloitte Ross Tohmatsu from practicing under the Deloitte name in the U.K. In England, DRT now practices under the name of Touche Ross.

For months, the bad news rolled into the Deloitte Ross Tohmatsu camp in waves. One after another, Deloitte practices in Belgium, France and Australia broke ranks, joining the stampede to Coopers. The results were devastating, making the would-be merger a nightmare for true believers Cook and Kangas and the subject of considerable amusement for their Big Six competitors.

During this period, Cook and Kangas grew testy. They

retreated from the press and displayed impatience with each other. How, Kangas wondered, could Cook have mis-judged his overseas practice to this extent? His mood vac-illated from agony to anger, with the latter directed at John Bullock, Deloitte U.K.'s managing partner, Coopers & Ly-brand and Mike Cook himself.

Although Cook and Kangas claimed they had discussed the possibility of U.K. defection from the start of their merger talks and had agreed to proceed with the union even if the split did occur, both men had to wonder at this point (if not out loud, then to themselves) if their grand scheme would succeed. "Shortly after Deloitte's British firm announced that they would not merge, we faced a critical meeting of our joint international executive com-mittee in Paris," Kangas said. "At this point, the situation was tense. The U.K. firm came to the meeting, trying to break up the merger by enticing others to join them. In everything they did, the Coopers & Lybrand partners were acting superaggressive, working behind the scenes to sign up more firms. Frankly, I was worried—very worried. At this juncture, the merger was in jeopardy, and I knew it.

"But fortunately, just as we hit bottom, things began to improve. Feeling themselves under fire from outsiders, the member firms actually pulled together, convinced that they could and should make the merger work. It was a turning point, a galvanizing experience for all of us."

Still, a Deloitte Ross Tohmatsu without Deloitte's U.K. and Dutch practices was a substantially weaker version of the Big Six power Cook and Kangas had had in mind when they decided to join forces. More than anything else, the crumbling of the original DRT master plan gave credence to the argument that megamergers would put undue stress on the firms, reducing rather than reinforcing their ability to practice as professionals—a tune Peter Scanlon had been singing ever since the game of musical chairs began in earnest.

"When I looked around and saw the other firms merging, I asked myself, 'Should we do the same?' Scanlon said. "The answer was 'No.' Why? Because I couldn't identify a weakness in our practice that a megamerger would fill. Also, change of that magnitude always brings trauma to a professional firm, and I saw no credible reason to endure that kind of trauma."

Criticized as a closed-minded leader whose isolationist policies would take a heavy toll on Coopers as it tried to compete against the new breed of megafirms, Scanlon nevertheless held fast, reiterating his belief that shotgun mergers would create bigger but not necessarily better or more profitable accounting firms. In standing pat while his peers rushed to the altar, Scanlon was betting that in the end the market would go his way. Events have proved him to be extremely lucky, extremely wise—or a bit of both.

In the aftermath of the defections from DRT—its components scattered all over Europe—Coopers emerged with the biggest accounting practices in Britain, Germany and the Netherlands. In the United Kingdom alone—once projected to be a DRT stronghold—Coopers wound up number one in the rankings, surpassing the previous market leader, Peat Marwick. Without the fanfare of a megamerger, without a flurry of press releases, without slick brochures announcing itself, as Deloitte & Touche did, "The Ideal Firm," Coopers managed to bolster its worldwide practice, achieving something the "master plan" mergers may never do.

Today, the Big Six are an amalgam of recently merged firms and those that remain more or less independent. Just which will fare better over the long run is open to question, but early returns indicate that the mergers have turned off the very clients they were supposed to impress. In a 1989 survey of *Fortune* 1,000 financial executives, *Bowman's Accounting Report* found that nearly two thirds of the respondents insisted that the mergers were not good for clients. Of those whose auditing firms had merged, more than 25 percent revealed that they would consider changing auditors. "Mergers reduce competition, which in the long run only results in inefficiencies," one client commented. Another said, "We see zero advantages to us from the merger of E&Y, and there are some disadvantages. All of the firms are still alike—they all send green people to be trained and offer little or no value added from the audit process. We get more benefit from our own people by far."

Interestingly, the four horsemen that have not merged with their peers—Arthur Andersen, Coopers & Lybrand, Price Waterhouse and Peat Marwick—commanded the highest ratings in the survey. If the CPAs are willing to listen, they may find that there is a message in all of this.

"No matter how the firms trumpet these mergers," Art Bowman said, "from the clients' perspective they are done more for the betterment of the partners than for the betterment of the clients. The simple fact is that clients want service, and they don't buy the line that they're going to get more of that when two firms join into one. In many cases, they think that just the opposite is true.

"The firms are out of step with their clients. They're so busy declaring that they are, or will be, the largest practices in the world that they don't hear the clients saying, 'Who cares? After a certain point, how big do you have to be?' "

6

BEHIND CLOSED DOORS

How the Big Six Compete for Clients

If a single factor decides which Big Six firms will remain in the privileged caste at the top of the profession, which will continue to grow and which will fall by the wayside, it is the all-important "proposal process." Shrouded in mystery, shielded from public view, this is accounting's version of trench warfare, in which the firms battle for the right to represent clients contemplating a change of auditors.

Nothing is more important to the Big Six than their performance in the proposal process. It is here where all the firms' resources are focused on the single-minded pursuit of new clients. All of the marketing mechanisms installed in the past decade (the practice niches, the multinational networks, the elevation of rainmaking partners) are only extra baggage unless they translate into new business.

The question is, how are the various firms faring in the crucible of the proposal process? Which appear to have mastered the process, and which appear to be struggling with it? One way to gain insight into that process is to peer through the keyhole at two hotly contested audit engagements that took place recently, to see why the losers lost and the winners prevailed. Although any proposal process is generally off limits to all but senior corporate officers and the audit firms bidding for their business, here is a behind-the-scenes look at the presentations and the deliberations in these two competitions. While they must be viewed as a random sample of the firms' performances, they offer rare insights into the process that can make or break even the most prestigious accounting firm.

COMPETITION I: THE BATTLE FOR
A CONSUMER-PRODUCTS GIANT

The battle began when the client, a bedrock of the U.S. corporate community, decided to entertain proposals from outside auditors for the first time in more than six decades. Previous to that, Coopers & Lybrand had reigned unchallenged as the company's guardian of the balance sheet. For Coopers, the relationship had brought permanence, prestige and substantial fees that rose virtually unchallenged year after year. In other words, it was a dream client. But it was one that was now in jeopardy as management, which had initiated a companywide process of evaluating all of its vendor relationships, was calling in other firms to see how they stacked up in terms of service and fees.

In these fishing expeditions, the incumbent auditor starts off with a built-in advantage. As a "member of the family," it can stress the benefits of a continuing relationship. There is some substance to that claim. Incumbent auditors are familiar with the company's operations and the caliber of its internal controls; by the same token, client personnel are familiar with the auditors and are accustomed to working with them. Maintaining the status quo spares the company a disruptive transition from one audit firm to another.

To capitalize on this advantage, the current auditor must demonstrate a level of client commitment a newcomer is unlikely to match. But here, Coopers & Lybrand dropped the ball. Yes, the firm stated in writing and in person that this bedrock client was important to Coopers, but it failed to go beyond the verbal boilerplate that is as predictable and heartfelt as a form letter. Caught up in the commercialization that has swept through the Big Six, prompting the firms to discard the gentlemanly practices of the past, Coopers forgot just how important the personal touch can be in retaining long-term engagements. Although an appearance by Coopers' chairman, Peter Scanlon, would hardly have sewed up the account, his absence throughout the proposal process raised a question about the firm's commitment to the client, a feeling underscored by the fact that Deloitte's chairman, Mike Cook, and Peat Marwick's managing partner, Larry Horner, found time to make personal appearances on behalf of their firms.

"If seeing my face has any impact on choosing an auditor," Scanlon said, "then something is wrong with the process." Although he may be right, his failure to squeeze one of the firm's oldest clients into his itinerary took a heavy toll on Coopers' prospects.

At the outset, each of the Big Six firms was invited to propose for the client, but in short order the competition boiled down to three serious contenders—Peat Marwick, Coopers and Arthur Andersen. Of these, three factors weighed in Peat Marwick's favor from the start. Considering that this was a multinational engagement involving the audit of dozens of overseas subsidiaries, Peat appeared to have a leg up on the competition. The firm's successful merger with KMG Main Hurdman gave it a strong international network composed of prominent accounting firms throughout Western Europe. And having consummated that merger two years before (in 1987), Peat had put the turmoil and instability of mergermania behind it. For the immediate future, it was likely to be a stable practice.

It was also skillful at the proposal process. Although the accounting profession has grown increasingly sales-oriented, a great number of practitioners have remained inveterate closet cases, more comfortable in the company of computer printouts than onstage before an audience of prospective clients. But it is here where Peat excelled. Armed with sophisticated visuals and led by partners who were skilled at creating a sense of theater, they had learned how to command the spotlight, sometimes making those who followed them look like amateurs.

Such was the case with the client at hand. So strong was Peat's performance that it would have won the engagement hands down had a vote been taken as soon as the curtain closed on its presentation. Sensing the positive feedback from the client's auditor selection committee, Peat's partners strode from the room, confident that this one was in the bag.

Little did they know that their overseas affiliates, touted as the secret weapon in the Peat Marwick worldwide practice, would wind up blowing the deal. This surprising turn of events came into focus as the client's overseas subsidiaries rated the teams of Big Six auditors that had called on them as part of the proposal process.

Almost unanimously, the subs were unimpressed with

Peat, ranking the firm third behind Coopers and Andersen in overall capabilities. From the client's perspective, it was an unacceptable weakness in the Peat system. Because this was truly a multinational audit (roughly 60 percent of the clients' sales were generated overseas), an engagement team that left more than half its constituents cold was simply unacceptable. Peat's European partners had proved to be an Achilles heel that no domestic presentation, regardless of its strength, could overcome. Peat was out of it.

The spotlight now fell on the incumbent, Coopers & Lybrand. With all of the Big Six now claiming that they go beyond the attest function by bringing a "businessman's perspective" to their audits, a key feature of the formal proposals is a series of recommendations for making improvements in the client's business. These strategies are specifically designed to impress management that the firm will bring value added over and beyond the audit opinion.

Here, Coopers was at a disadvantage. While the contenders for the engagement could make all kinds of marvelous promises, the incumbent was going to be judged by its real-world performance. If it had treated the client as an annuity—if it had done little more than sign the audit opinion—its failure to provide value added would become abundantly clear at this stage of the game, a sticky wicket Coopers found itself trapped in.

When the client heard Peat Marwick and Arthur Andersen make insightful recommendations about their business, members of the selection committee asked such questions as "Where the hell has Coopers been all these years? Why didn't they bring similar ideas to our attention? Were they sleeping? Did they take us for granted?

"Oh sure, they put some recommendations in their proposal too, but these were issues we'd raised first. They just took the opportunity to boomerang them back to us. Judged on this basis alone, why the hell didn't we fire their asses years ago?"

But Coopers' problems didn't end there. Over the years, the firm had increased its fees on an annual basis, using a percentage factor that failed to consider competitive rates. This practice, lucrative as it is, carries a built-in time bomb. Inevitably, the day of reckoning comes.

For Coopers, that day came midway through the proposal process. With competitors now bidding for the engagement, Coopers' fee of roughly $1.8 million was a sitting duck. Clearly, the firm was caught between a rock and a hard place. If it held fast to its $1.8 million fee, it would be badly undercut by competitors; if it made the necessary cuts, it would be accused of having overcharged for years.

In the end, Coopers opted to cut its fee to about $1.45 million, hoping this would keep it in the running for the engagement. But it only drove another nail into the coffin. "If Coopers & Lybrand can make money auditing us for $400,000 less than they're charging now, that just tells me they've been sticking it to us," complained an audit committee member. "Where I come from, we don't like to do business with people like that."

Even with its reduced fee, Coopers remained the high bidder, coming in slightly over Peat Marwick's $1.4 million and holding an embarrassingly wide margin over a bid that would soon be put on the table by Arthur Andersen. It was a curious strategy for Coopers & Lybrand. As the incumbent auditor for an old-line client, Coopers had the inside track. The boards of such blue-chip companies may allow reviews of auditors (just to keep everyone on his toes), but when push comes to shove they are reluctant to authorize a switch unless there is a compelling reason to do so. In the absence of gross negligence (which Coopers was not guilty of) or a wide gap in quoted fees, the incumbent will often retain the engagement even if the competition appears to hold an advantage in technical prowess or industry experience.

Which is why Coopers' behavior was so surprising. By making it clear that it would match all quotes, Coopers would have neutralized the competition, virtually guaranteeing its continuity on the engagement. But instead the firm remained at the high end of the fee curve.

Two factors played a role here. First, Coopers knew that the more it cut from its current fee, the more it would appear to have pigged out in the past. Slashing about $400,000 from the bill was uncomfortable enough; dropping the charge by a greater amount would be difficult to explain. Thus Coopers' dilemma: Every dollar it volunteered to subtract from its current fee made it look all the more like a glutton caught with its fingers in the pie.

Second, Coopers knew from past experience that there is always a reservoir of support for the incumbent firm. In spite of failures and omissions by the current auditor, a majority of the selection committee inevitably takes the position that "the devil we know is preferable to the devil we don't know."

In light of the fact that most of the decision makers active in this case had known only one audit firm for their entire careers and had thus come to consider the incumbents as "part of the family," Coopers apparently believed its allies on the selection committee would swing the vote in its favor. With this scenario in mind, the $1.45 million quote was most likely intended as a compromise to show that the firm was responsive to competition (while still assuring itself a cushy margin on the audit). Wise or not, this was the bid Coopers put on the table.

Had the competition been limited to Peat and Coopers,

chances are that Coopers' strategy would have prevailed. In spite of the fact that the selection committee perceived Peat Marwick as better suited for the engagement, and in spite of the fact that Coopers' high fees and less than stellar service had left a bitter taste in the client's mouth, the CFO was not about to recommend a change in auditors unless the move brought a substantial reduction in fees. With Coopers having virtually matched Peat Marwick, there was little incentive to switch to the latter, especially in light of Peat's poor ratings from the overseas subsidiaries.

But the real threat to Coopers came not from Peat, but from Arthur Andersen. Fresh from the humiliating experience of having its highly publicized merger talks with Price Waterhouse dead-end in full view of the client community, Andersen (much like Deloitte after its star-crossed merger attempt with Price Waterhouse) came out of the ruins set on proving to the world that it had no need for a merger partner anyway. With Coopers' client one of the first it would propose for as a confirmed independent, Andersen was determined to succeed by unleashing an impressive array of professional resources.

From the beginning, Andersen outmaneuvered the competition. With the client headquartered in a modest-sized city near Chicago, every other auditor competing for its business took the predictable route, suggesting that the engagement be based in the "windy city," where it could tap the resources of a major practice office. But in a shrewd move, Andersen capitalized on its strength in the client's hometown by proposing to base the audit there rather than in Chicago. With this critical decision, Andersen positioned itself as the one firm offering a closer, more intimate relationship with the client. "If there's a problem, we can be at your offices in half an hour," an Andersen partner assured the selection committee. "Our competition can't make that claim."

But the real benefit of Andersen's site selection proposal accrued to Andersen rather than to the client. With the audit process widely viewed as a commodity service that is virtually identical from firm to firm, Andersen proposed the local setting as a way to differentiate itself from the competition. While Peat and Coopers relied on the old saws about audit quality and proficiency, Andersen offered a tangible difference the client could relate to.

All of the major components of Andersen's proposal meshed in a convincing presentation, not just in writing but in real-world performance. Where Peat's overseas squads had left the client cold, Andersen's created a strong impression. Office by office, subsidiary by subsidiary, client management described the Andersen team calling on them as active, knowledgeable and of the highest caliber.

Andersen's success in the field was a clear tribute to its unique strengths as an international practice. Of all the Big Six, it is the only firm with a truly unified practice world-wide. As much as Andersen's competitors claim to practice as "one firm" on a global basis, they are mostly collections of affiliated firms operating as far-flung franchises. Not so at Andersen. Unlike the other firms, which built their over-seas practices through the franchise system, Andersen's international firm had been built brick by brick, with Andersen people opening the offices, launching the firms and training the personnel. From the beginning, Andersen professionals from all over the world trained together at St. Charles and coordinated their work and their finances through the firm's Swiss-based headquarters, Société Co-opérative. This has given them a unity of mission and an esprit de corps unmatched by their competitors.

But in spite of Andersen's strengths if the engagement were to be awarded solely on the basis of professional competence and client-partner chemistry, choosing between Peat and Andersen would have been difficult. Although Andersen scored points internationally as well as with its plan to center the audit in the client's hometown, Peat enjoyed the stability of a fully consummated merger while Andersen was still reeling from the effects of its accountant/consultant conflict. Adding it all up, Andersen did hold an advantage over Peat, but not enough to tip the scales away from Coopers. At least until the client factored in the all-important matter of fees. Here Andersen seized command, preempting Peat and Coopers with a bid of $850,000.

The strategy was brilliant. By entering the contest with a rock-bottom quote that knocked about $1 million from Coopers' current-year fee, Andersen recognized that it would be pulling the rug out from under those committee members intent on retaining the incumbent for sentimental reasons. Were there to be parity (or something close to it) between Coopers and the challengers, financial management would have been hard pressed to sever a long-term audit relationship in spite of its deficiencies. But with Andersen's fee promising substantial savings, the book was closed on sentimentality, loyalty and all the other trappings of annuity relationships.

Days before the three contenders were scheduled to make their final presentations to the client, the selection committee assembled to review the process to date. Within minutes, it was clear that Andersen had the engagement locked up. "The sense I'm getting here is that every person in this room wants Arthur Andersen to be named as our auditor," said a vice president in attendance. "Does anyone differ with me on that?"

A silence fell over the room.

Although the formalities would continue as scheduled, from that moment on Andersen had won the contest, outclassing Peat Marwick and replacing Coopers & Lybrand after two generations as the company's auditors.

COMPETITION II: THE POWER OF INCUMBENCY

At just about the same time that Arthur Andersen was making life miserable for Coopers & Lybrand, one of Andersen's own annuity relationships was coming unglued. A major charitable organization had opened its audit to competition after more than two decades of loyalty to Andersen. The goal: to reduce the current $1.4 million audit fee without sacrificing the quality work management believed it had received from Andersen over the years.

As the contest began in the spring of 1989, all the giant firms were considered candidates for the audit and were invited to submit statements of qualifications. But soon after the documents were received, the merger announcement by Ernst & Whinney and Arthur Young knocked those two out of the box. Recognizing that E&Y would be entering a disruptive period, the client opted to remove the firm from contention.

Two other firms, Coopers and Touche Ross, were just as easy to eliminate. Although both claimed to have strong nonprofit experience, their credentials in this highly specialized field appeared relatively weak. This was too much of a handicap to overcome. High-visibility charitable organizations must remain squeaky clean, free of even the taint of fraud. A single news story charging misappropriation of funds can lead to a precipitous decline in donations, thus cutting off the lifeblood of the organization. Mindful of this threat, the committee members knew their auditors had to be at the cutting edge of nonprofit practice.

By early summer, the losers were given the bad news and the four finalists—Price Waterhouse, Deloitte Haskins & Sells, Peat Marwick and incumbent Arthur Andersen— were invited to submit formal proposals by early October. This left ample time for the firms to visit the charity's headquarters and field offices, meet with personnel, gauge audit risk, plan audit scope and put all of the resulting programs and observations into four-color, professionally printed proposals that would serve as the centerpiece of their marketing efforts. If all went according to plan, the charity's selection committee would receive four written proposals and listen to four accompanying oral presentations, using this as the basis for making the final decision: whether to appoint a new auditor or retain Arthur Andersen.

But as is typical in auditor reviews, the process quickly veered from the carefully structured plan the client had created to an unexpected free-for-all. Soon after Ernst & Young was dropped from consideration on the grounds that it was embarking on a potentially disruptive merger, Price Waterhouse announced that it was holding hands with Arthur Andersen, and Deloitte revealed its plan to fuse with Touche Ross. With three of the finalists now merger candidates, why, Ernst & Young partners called to ask, should they not be considered as well?

Behind the scenes, a senior Ernst & Young partner asked for a chance to get back into the race. Though the client toyed with the idea, the request was denied. With the review process already under way, and with the selection committee determined to simplify rather than complicate the auditor selection, E&Y was rebuffed.

At this point, another would-be candidate tried to wedge its way into the competition. Hoping to capitalize on a relationship with a member of the charity's management team, the accounting firm of BDO Seidman sent a "please consider us" letter (accompanied by a sketchy statement of qualifications) to the selection committee. Seidman is a standing member of the so-called second tier that sits below the Big Six in the hierarchy of major accounting/consulting firms. Although dwarfed by the Big Six, the second-tier firms are capable of servicing all but the largest multinational audits. With forty offices and two thousand professionals throughout the United States, Seidman was clearly in a position to handle the audit of this domestic charitable organization.

But in spite of Seidman's capabilities, it was locked out of the market. Just as the *Fortune* 100 rarely depart from their preference for Big Six audits, the charity's selection committee limited its competition to the same clique of accounting behemoths, not because the Big Six stand for superior professional standards (they do not), but because the world has stamped a "Good Housekeeping Seal of Approval" on their audits. No matter what goes wrong with the audit, no one can ever accuse the client of choosing a fly-by-night CPA firm. "Don't blame us," they can say. "We picked one of the premier firms in the profession."

There was no way BDO Seidman was going to break through that barrier. The firm's letter of introduction was virtually ignored. As BDO Seidman probably knew from the start, this engagement was the private preserve of the accounting behemoths.

In September the finalists submitted written proposals to the charity's world headquarters. Predictably, the documents were adorned with condescending tributes to the prospective client.

From Price Waterhouse's chairman Shaun O'Malley: "Let me take this opportunity to express my thanks to your committee for selecting us to submit our proposal. . . . In addition to the on-the-job commitment of our people, you can expect a significant commitment to volunteer activities. Price Waterhouse staff have an outstanding record of achievement as volunteers for community and charitable organizations. I will personally encourage our partners and staff throughout the country to build on this record."

From Arthur Andersen's Larry Weinbach: "While other firms may claim to rival us in commitment and competence, no firm can claim or demonstrate the continuity, the in-depth knowledge of your operations and the commitment to the cause . . . that we have annually demonstrated to you."

Judging by these and similar pledges of loyalty from the other contenders, one would have thought the Big Six were so committed to philanthropy that they were donating their services free of charge. Far from it. While all of the firms bent over backwards to picture themselves as a new generation of Albert Schweitzers, they were viewing the engagement as a profit-making opportunity. To the contenders, this was pure business.

In reviewing the formal proposals, the selection committee detected distinctions between the firms, some subtle, some dramatic: Deloitte Haskins & Sells appeared relatively weak. For a firm that prided itself on the Mike Cook–style of thorough preparation and savvy salesmanship, the DH&S proposal was a disappointment. As perceived by the committee, the audit plan was unimpressive, the text showed little insight into the way the charity ran its operations and there was little in the way of a businessman's perspective. The impression was that of a slapdash proposal from a firm diverted by the problems and logistics of a pending merger with Touche Ross.

In terms of fees, Deloitte's quote of $984,000 was competitive but in no way low enough to compensate for its weak proposal. Reflecting Cook's strong feeling that quality, value-added audits can command substantial fees, the proposal stated, "We disagree with those in our industry who regard the audit as a commodity. As a DH&S client, you will receive a high-quality, cost-effective audit of your financial statements. But our services will go far beyond perfunctory attest functions. In the course of conducting our audits, we fully expect to develop information and insights concerning your operations that will be of direct value."

All well and good, but promising valuable insights is one thing; delivering them is another. Considering that Deloitte raised the issue of value added, it was obligated to support its claims with concrete suggestions on how it would go beyond the "perfunctory attest functions." But it failed to do so and was never viewed as a serious contender.

As Price Waterhouse entered the competition, its reputation as the carriage-trade accounting firm turned out to be a handicap. The client wondered—correctly—if it could compete for attention with the blue-chip clientele that had always been PW's pride and joy. Faced with this question, PW faced an uphill battle.

But give Price Waterhouse an "A" for effort. From the written proposal all the way through to the in-person presentations, the firm tried valiantly to position itself as the ideal auditors for the nonprofit sector. In visits to the client's facilities around the United States, the PW team demonstrated an enthusiasm and commitment that impressed local managers, most of whom gave the firm high

marks. Unlike Deloitte, which only promised a businessman's perspective, Price delivered, listing meaningful observations about the client's operations.

In spite of this impressive effort, two factors removed
Price Waterhouse from serious consideration. First, its attempts to picture itself as a pillar of the charitable community notwithstanding, the firm's identity as a Brahmin
of the corporate world came through. References listed in
the proposal included only a sprinkling of nonprofit clients
and even those—such as the Field Museum of Natural
History—were markedly dissimilar to the engagement at
hand.

Second, and most telling, Price Waterhouse quoted a
grossly inflated fee of $1,255,000, well in excess of its com-
petitors' bids. As the only finalist to cross the $1 million
threshold, PW gave credence to the fear that it was out of
touch with the cost-conscious world of nonprofit clients.

Peat Marwick's proposal was strong on all fronts. Its
nonprofit practice featured a long list of prominent clients,
and the firm's top nonprofit partner was nationally known.
Furthermore, its audit plan (as spelled out in the proposal)
won high marks with the selection committee. To ice the
issue, Peat's quote of $950,000 was the lowest of the
challengers'.

As is typical of the incumbent auditor, Arthur Andersen
played on the client's sympathies, appealing to those factions that resist change of any kind. Titling its proposal
"The Benefits of a Continuing Relationship," Andersen
took out the violins, claiming that it considered the charity
". . . our premier not-for-profit client. . . . While other
firms may claim to rival us in commitment and competence,
no firm can claim or demonstrate the continuity, the in-
depth knowledge of your operations, and the commitment
to the cause . . . that we have annually demonstrated to

you. We believe that the continuation of our professional relationship will provide you with exceptional competence, incomparable commitment and superior service at the lowest net cost. . . . This relationship should continue!"

Lowest net cost? That depended on who was adding the numbers. Andersen had fattened its fees to the charity year after year to the point that it was hardly competitive, a fact it would have to change if it wanted to retain the client. The "benefits of a continuing relationship" are important, but no one, not even the staunchest defenders of the status quo, will pay a king's ransom for it.

Just as Coopers recognized in dealing with its annuity client, the pressure on incumbents to become competitive poses all sorts of problems. After decades of monopolizing the account and charging premium fees, the prospect of relinquishing those fat margins is anathema. No doubt Andersen felt that way too. Its solution was to propose what appeared to be a competitive fee of $796,000, which reflected a $300,000 contribution Andersen would make to the charity. The hitch was that the lower fee would eliminate services performed in prior years—services Andersen claimed the competition was also omitting in their fee proposals. As Andersen noted in its proposal: "There are numerous services provided at the direction and the request of 'the client' . . . as part of our annual examinations that have been a component of the overall fee but not separately identified. . . . To ensure that our estimate is comparable with the estimates of our competitors, we have not reflected the cost of providing the non-base services . . . in our estimate."

What Andersen failed to mention was that its fees were based on a 15 percent hourly rate reduction for nonprofit clients compared to a 35 percent discount offered by the challengers. On an engagement of this size, the differential amounted to a substantial sum. While Andersen's discount totaled $299,000, Peat's weighed in at $483,000. Andersen's offer to make a $300,000 cash contribution to the charity seemed to be a way of making up for its paltry per-hour discount without appearing to reduce its rate in the face of competition. Although Andersen may have thought this was a brilliant strategy, it hardly impressed the client. In this review, the incumbent's position appeared uncertain.

As the process came down to its final days, the contenders were scheduled to make personal appearances before the client's selection committee. Typically, these face-to-face meetings are conducted in a biased environment, with the client already leaning toward a particular auditor. But in this case, the competition remained wide open. Although Price and Deloitte were long shots, Peat and Andersen were neck and neck. What was more, the members of the committee appeared sufficiently open-minded that an outstanding presentation by any one of the firms might put it over the top.

On the day scheduled, the four contenders were allowed an hour each. First on the agenda was Price Waterhouse, which assembled a high-ranking team headlined by chairman O'Malley. As PW launched into its spiel, two things were apparent from the start. In spite of its historic orientation toward the Exxons and the IBMs of the corporate world, PW really wanted this engagement to vanquish its would-be merger partner Arthur Andersen. Now that they had gone their separate ways, both sides were determined to vanquish each other—to prove to themselves and to the world that they were the stronger member of the aborted merger. Winning here would be more than a victory; it would be revenge.

But as hard as the PW team tried to impress the client,

the selection committee couldn't help but recognize that the firm was trapped in its elitist traditions. Seated stiffly behind a dais, looking like wooden figures trying to figure out what they were supposed to be doing, the PW partners appeared uncomfortable in the role of salesmen. Rather than subtly trying to position themselves as the right professionals for the job, they lectured the committee, informing them in so many words that they would be fortunate to have Price Waterhouse as their auditors.

PW's presentation came across as poorly planned and amateurish—even the offer to cut its fee. Having gotten wind that its fee was way out of line, O'Malley proceeded to level the playing field: "We're so interested in your choosing the best firm and in removing the issue of fees from the deliberations, that we're willing to reduce our fee to match the incumbent."

As far as Price Waterhouse was concerned, this was a magnanimous offer; to the selection committee, it was a case of a high-handed firm simply getting competitive. In the end, the fee reduction did nothing but reinforce PW's elitist image. By the time O'Malley and Company marched from the conference room, their fate was sealed. They had lost this one.

Next up to bat was Deloitte Haskins & Sells, whose presentation (if it could be called that) looked as though it had been patched together the night before. For starters, Deloitte's regional vice chairman admitted that he didn't have much in the way of a formal presentation. He would, however, be willing to answer questions from the selection committee. To those assembled, his remarks sounded like this: "Hey guys, we'd like to get this engagement (who doesn't want a big new client?), but we're not about to expend much effort on your behalf."

Accompanied by a skeleton team of three underlings

(including an auditor who looked too young to be out of school), the vice chairman fielded questions with charm and authority but could hardly make up for the firm's lack of preparation or for the conspicuous absence of Touche Ross, which had just agreed to merge with Deloitte. Asked why Touche partners hadn't joined in the presentation, the Deloitte executive did his best to gloss over the issue, claiming that the Deloitte team would handle the engagement at the outset but would be joined by the Touche people over time.

This was begging the issue. The failure to include a Touche component in the presentation reflected poorly on Deloitte's assessment of its new partners, and on the firm's progress in merging the practices. Bottom line: This embarrassingly weak presentation left Deloitte without a prayer. It was out of the running.

Peat Marwick's presentation was the Academy Award winner. Unlike the stuffy Price Waterhouse team, which had hidden behind the dais, and unlike the Deloitte contingent, which had allowed the client to take the lead, the Peat Marwick cast put on a show, worked the room, circled the horseshoe conference table and used charts, diagrams and videos to sell, sell, sell. When the presentation was complete, Peat had reinforced its position as a major contender. Judging by the self-confident air of the Peat partners, they thought they had this engagement sewn up.

But Arthur Andersen was still to be heard from. Based on the usual standards, Andersen's performance gave Peat little to worry about. Looking rather disheveled in a wrinkled suit, an Andersen partner appeared uncomfortable before the committee. Leaning against a desk and fidgeting with a pen, he gave a canned speech complete with an overused chart that ranks Andersen as the highest-rated firm among college professors. That this had zero credibility off campus didn't stop the partner from building it into his presentation.

After this lackluster performance, Andersen fielded questions from the committee members, most of whom were curious about the firm's sudden willingness to slash its fees. Between the lines, the committee was posing embarrassing questions: Had Andersen overcharged the charity through the years, levying enormous fees because it viewed the client as an annuity? Had it capitalized unfairly on a long-term relationship? Had it violated a sacred trust?

No, no, no, Andersen claimed. Nothing of the kind. We lavished extensive services on you and were merely paid fairly for our work. The fee would be reduced now, they insisted, only because the client had asked all of the contenders to bid on an audit of a more limited scope.

Convincing? Not exactly. Andersen's defensive attitude did more to confuse the fee issue than to set it straight. To compound matters, the firm's presentation was not compelling enough to shift the focus from fees to performance. And so, awkwardly, the Andersen presentation sputtered to a halt. After the obligatory chitchat with the committee members, the partners filed out of the room, leaving the charity to decide which of the four contenders would win the engagement.

On the surface, Peat Marwick appeared to have the inside track. Its nonprofit practice had made the most compelling presentation. From all indications, it was the favorite. But in the competition for Big Six audits, appearances can be misleading. In this case, an invisible factor figured more prominently in the ultimate decision than anything revealed in the long and intensive review process. It was the inclination of a company or an institution to resist change.

The sentiment for retaining Andersen as the client's auditors proved strongest in the charity's divisional offices that had worked with Andersen for decades and that were dead set against switching horses at this point. Writing to headquarters executives, divisional personnel had done their best to influence the outcome in favor of Andersen. One wrote, "Throughout the discussion of our relationship with the auditors, it was evident that the committee [an advisory committee apart from the auditor selection committee] felt a remarkable kinship to Arthur Andersen. . . . Further, everyone at the meeting concurred; the difficulty we would face if, heaven forbid, we did make a change, would be a burden. . . . Arthur Andersen is a useful, competent friend. We ought not forget that." Another commented, "These people from Arthur Andersen have become friends and (almost) colleagues. They serve us well. And there is nothing wrong with that."

As the review process had moved through its various stages, a groundswell of support for retaining Andersen moved from the divisional level to the national headquarters and ultimately to the selection committee. Soon enough, it would overshadow all other considerations, propelling the incumbent into the number-one position.

When the vote was taken, Andersen had the majority. It retained the engagement not because it had outperformed the others but because it had provided satisfactory service over the years, because it agreed to compromise on fees and, most important, because it was a known quantity.

The committee members were intelligent, hardworking volunteers intent on making the right decision. In this case, the inertia of a continuing relationship moved them to vote for the incumbent. It didn't always work that way: Witness Coopers & Lybrand's loss of the consumer products company after sixty-plus years of service. But when the incumbent auditor makes a concerted effort to keep the client, when it plays on the theme of continuity while getting competitive with fees, it is hard to unseat.

The power of incumbency makes a mockery of some of the biggest audit selection contests. Even in those cases where the incumbent has a clear advantage to the extent that it is likely to retain the engagement no matter what the others do, the competing firms continue to fly in rain-makers, to produce costly videos, to prepare elaborate pro-posals and to jump through whatever hoops the prospective client puts in their path—all on the slim chance that they will defy the odds and come away the winner.

This is the nasty underside of the audit business, Big Six–style. The days when clients called on a single firm to discuss an audit relationship because that firm had the requisite image or best credentials are long gone. Today the most venerable names in a once-pristine profession are reduced to common vendors, scratching for business like the salesmen they still snub their noses at.

"Look, most of us went into this career to be professional accountants, not professional pitchmen," said Steve Op-penheim. "If we'd wanted to sell, we would have gone to work for Brooks Brothers. Of course, accountants always had to attract clients. But in the past, the firms sought to do that on the basis of their skills. Now they rely on their pitch. In doing so, they've forgotten that as accountants, it's all right to be for hire, but it's not all right to be for sale."

EPILOGUE

A t the very same time that mergers were reducing the Big Eight to a Big Six, rumors were swirling through the profession that additional unions would soon shrink the oligopoly to a Big Four. Once the mating dance was set in motion, the theory went, it would continue until each of the firms had found a partner.

Looking to the months ahead, this is unlikely. The firms that have merged are still absorbing the effects of combining far-flung organizations. And those that have remained independent have a stake in staying their current course. Price Waterhouse hardly wants to strike out three times; Peat Marwick got more (or less) than it bargained for with the Main Hurdman KMG acquisition (many of the Main Hurdman partners had to be axed); Arthur Andersen is more convinced than ever that it is superior to the other firms; and Coopers & Lybrand, while maintaining an antimerger posture, has already benefited from defections overseas.

Does this mean that the Big Six configuration will hold steady for generations to come? Absolutely not. These are firms in flux, in crisis and in constant pursuit of strategies and alliances that will give them a competitive advantage. All of the drive, ambition and egotistical empire building that prompted the current reordering at the top of the accounting profession remain as strong as ever. Deny it as they do, every one of the firms is still hell-bent on growth for the sake of growth, on vanquishing its peers for the thrill of victory, on expanding its practice in every direction and, above all else, on being known as "the largest firm in the Big Six. The giant of giants."

Considering this expansionary psychology, which is now deeply embedded in all of the firms, new mergers are bound to occur by the mid-1990s. As they have done in the past, managing partners will initiate the process, making passes at their counterparts: an informal gesture at first, perhaps small talk at a cocktail party. But gradually the idea will take hold, leading to serious talks and an announcement that two of the firms—sworn to independence only months before—are headed for the altar.

If any such union would throw fear into the hearts of the assembled, it is a merger between Peat Marwick and Arthur Andersen. As the reigning giants before the current spate of megamergers was consummated, Peat and Andersen came to think of their firms as being in a class by themselves: the Big Two. The prospect of joining forces to create the Big One may be so attractive as to overcome the preference for going it alone. Were the merger to occur, a new wave of Big Six combinations would likely follow. To what extent the Justice Department would allow so much power to be concentrated in the hands of a few firms is open to question. But even a laissez-faire administration would be forced to draw the line if competition was so limited that a handful of auditors could set fees and policies at will.

Beyond the issue of size, the firms must face a more serious question: What, exactly, do they want to be? For generations, the Big Eight were proud of their role as audit professionals, serving as critical checks and balances on the accuracy of corporate financial statements. The fact that they were well paid (but not wealthy) partners in collegial practices that stressed caution, prudence and a disdain for the trappings of commercial businesses was a matter of pride.

Today, just the opposite is true. Anything that smacks of this traditional outlook is dismissed as a relic of the past. Although auditing still generates the bulk of Big Six revenues, it has taken a back seat to consulting in terms of growth, glamour and profitability. What's more, as the audit practices have become tainted by the S&L scandal and its attendant litigation, management views the audit as a legal time bomb with the potential to wreak financial havoc in the firms. With this in mind, managing partners are placing ever-greater emphasis on consulting.

As the firms become more intimately involved with their clients through their consulting practices, as they think of themselves more and more as consultants who happen to do audits just to get a foot in the door and as they continue to reward salesmanship and marketing over technical proficiency, they are clearly headed toward a day of reckoning—a day when the firms, or Congress acting for them, will force the issue and demand that they decide whether they want to retain the licensed privilege of auditing the corporate community by spinning off the MAS practices, or whether they want to join in the open competition of management consulting by ejecting the audit practices.

One thing is certain: By pursuing nonstop growth and expansion and by stretching the outside of the practice envelope, they are acting as their own worst enemies, moving swiftly toward a time when they cannot have it both ways. Within two decades, the Big Six, as we know it today, will more than likely cease to exist.

The years ahead promise to be trying for the professionals in the big accounting firms. As the financial toll from the

S&L fiasco continues to mount, and as legislators and their constituents continue to lay blame for much of the carnage on the auditors, the designation "certified public accountant" will lose much of the prestige and the aura of unquestioned integrity long associated with it. For the men and women who call themselves CPAs, this will be a wrenching experience, prompting many to reconsider their career decisions and others to abandon the profession entirely.

If declining status doesn't dissuade the best and brightest from joining the big accounting firms and entering the competition for partnerships, the threat of punishing litigation may do so. With the firms and in turn the partners in them liable for enormous lawsuits resulting from the S&L crisis and other cases of audit failure, the specter of financial ruin may well prompt the best prospects for the accounting profession to launch careers elsewhere. This could lead to a vicious cycle with poorly qualified individuals further reducing audit quality and producing a new spate of actions against the firms.

"It is theoretically possible that the accounting profession could go away—simply vanish," said Robert Levine, former CEO of the now bankrupt firm of Laventhol & Horwath. "If you look at the extent of the litigation the profession faces, you see that it could collapse under its own weight. When you add up the amount of money the firms may have to pay out in legal judgments and compare that to the amount of money they have, you see that there may not be enough to pay the piper.

"If legal payments don't kill the profession, it may die from the impact of good people leaving because they don't want to be personally vulnerable to huge legal settlements. Unless something is done to insulate the profession from the problems it faces, we could be an endangered species."

Levine's comments may prove to be prescient. Just months after sounding this warning, the beleaguered CEO presided over the collapse of his own firm, with seventh-ranked Laventhol falling victim to costly litigation and haphazard growth. The firm's demise was but one of a series of seismic shocks that jolted the profession and sent it reeling in the last months of 1990.

Soon after L&H succumbed to bankruptcy, another second-tier firm, New York's Spicer & Oppenheim, dissolved. Deeply wounded by the stock market crash of 1987, Spicer—which had been heavily dependent on the financial services industry—saw its finances deteriorate to the point that it was hard pressed to pay the rent on its World Trade Center headquarters. In a matter of months, partners from two once-proud and profitable firms were scurrying to find new jobs and, equally important, to protect their assets from creditors' claims.

Shock waves jolted the Big Six as well. Staging their second palace revolt in less than a decade, Peat Marwick partners turned back chairman Larry Horner's bid for re-election, choosing Jon Madonna, head of the firm's San Francisco office, to replace him. The revolt came in response to Horner's failure to select a popular running mate, to the partners' dissatisfaction with their earnings (a malaise that is spreading throughout the Big Six) and to a series of alleged management excesses outlined in a letter by a retired Peat partner.

Ernst & Young also took it on the chin. Just as Laventhol & Horwath and Spicer & Oppenheim were closing their doors, rumors swirled that liabilities arising from the S&L crisis would force E&Y into bankruptcy. Although the firm denied the rumors, in part by taking out full-page newspaper ads to tout its financial well-being, there was no denying that the costs of the S&L litigation may bring any number of Big Six firms to the brink of financial disaster.

Assuming a tidal wave of litigation forces the firms to close their doors, who would step in to fill the role of financial watchdogs? Although the giant CPA firms have left much to be desired in their role as guardians of the public interest, they have nevertheless served collectively as an independent check and balance on thousands of corporations and their executives. With the auditors absent from the scene, the public would lose its only means of confirming the accuracy of corporate financial statements. What's more, placing total responsibility for financial reporting in the hands of corporate managers would create a laissez-faire environment that in all likelihood would substantially increase the incidence of misleading and fraudulent reporting. Faith in the statements of public companies, in stock market investments, and ultimately in the capitalist system would deteriorate.

There are some who lack this faith now. Certainly the specter of the Big Six being swept into the vortex of the S&L scandal has contributed to that attitude. But as imperfect as the system of independent audits is today, it does provide a system of verification that is reasonably reliable in the vast majority of cases and contributes to an environment that discourages misleading or fraudulent reporting. For this to continue to be true, the audit firms will have to recognize the limitations inherent in their role as certified public accountants. By refocusing their efforts on professionalism, by having technical proficiency replace rainmaking as the most valued trait, they can improve audit quality and reliability, reduce the frequency of audit failure, diminish their vulnerability to punishing lawsuits and restore the profession's reputation as a bastion of honesty and integrity in a business world desperately in need of those traits.

To accomplish this, the firms will have to repudiate the drive toward unbridled growth that has dominated their cultures for two decades. In doing so, they will discover the wisdom in the now-famous line from Robert Browning's poem "Bishop Blougram's Apology": "Less is more."

INDEX

accounting firms:
auditing vs. consulting in,
19, 87–88, 105–12, 114–
122, 124–28, 140–42,
149, 152–53, 198, 251
client influence in, 195
compensation systems in,
129, 143–45
competition in, 20–21, 22,
50, 65, 86–87, 96–97,
109, 157–60, 178–79,
187–88
conflict of interest in, 113
identity crisis in, 18–24, 64
lowering of professional standards in, 66–68, 102
product vs. market orientation in, 23, 166
public interest
responsibility of, 21–22,
23–24, 41, 59–60, 61–
62, 67, 102, 254
review departments in, 103
see also specific firms
acquisitions, 17, 65, 127–28,
151*n*, 194
Adamuz N.V., 75
ADC loans, 66, 84–85, 87–88
advertising, 21, 141, 158, 253
aerospace industry, 18
Aetna Life & Casualty, 16

AICPA Audit and Accounting
Guide for Savings and
Loan Associations, 66,
83, 84
Allstate, 29
American Express, 17
American Institute of Certified
Public Accountants
(AICPA), 21, 43, 60, 83,
84, 158
Amir, Paul, 75, 77–78, 79, 96,
99–100
Andersen Consulting, 105–7,
123–24, 141–42, 151–
154, 197–99
Anderson, Bruce, 56
Apple Computer, 17
Arcady, Alex, 99
Arnett, Bob, 161–62
Arthur Andersen & Company,
56, 105–54, 163, 187,
192, 223, 250
accounting vs. consulting
divisions of, 19–20, 87–88,
105–12, 114–22, 124–
128, 140–42, 149, 152–
153, 198, 234
BHSL and, 86–89
Change Management Task
Force of, 141
competition for clients by,

Mark Stevens is the nation's foremost authority on America's giant accounting firms. He is also the founder of CPA Select, a Chappaqua, New York, firm that counsels Fortune 500 companies in the selection of independent auditors. In addition to being a nationally syndicated newspaper columnist and contributing editor of *M inc.* magazine, he has written more than a dozen books, including the best-selling *The Big Eight, The Accounting Wars,* and *Sudden Death: The Rise and Fall of E. F. Hutton,* which *Library Journal* named one of the best business books of the year.

DATE DUE

#7323394
4/15/95

PRINTED IN U.S.A.

HIGHSMITH 45-102